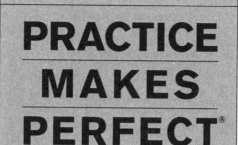

PRACTICE
MAKES
PERFECT®

Arabic
Vocabulary

Mahmoud Gaafar and Jane Wightwick

Mc
Graw
Hill

New York Chicago San Francisco Lisbon London Madrid Mexico City
Milan New Delhi San Juan Seoul Singapore Sydney Toronto

Contents

Introduction

You've done well to reach this far. Yes, it's the first line of the first paragraph, but you've probably decided you want to improve your Arabic vocabulary and figured practice and more practice is the best way to do just that. Keep adding layers of knowledge. We trust you will find this book useful in adding another layer or two. We have tried as much as possible to write a book that is fun to use.

In addition to the vocabulary and language content, *Practice Makes Perfect: Arabic Vocabulary* is dotted with a little cultural insight too. You'll come across little nuggets about Middle Eastern families, cooking, education, politics, crime, religion, and environment. You'll come across character types that seem vaguely familiar, like the politician who talks a lot but actually says nothing; or totally outrageous ones like the psychopath who strangles his neighbor to steal enough money to buy new curtains for his living room. Yes, this book is not for the faint-hearted!

What you won't find is a whole lot of cognates: words that have entered the Arabic vernacular from English. We didn't feel the need to tell you that "telescope" is تلسكوب or that "cinema" is سينما and that "granite" is جرانيت. Think of these cognates as bonus vocabulary and maybe keep a little separate notebook where you write these words whenever you come across them.

To get the most out of *Practice Makes Perfect: Arabic Vocabulary* you need to be able to read the script and to be comfortable with some basic Arabic. The text weaves in and out of both English and Arabic, and you need to be able to weave with it, at your own pace.

Practice Makes Perfect: Arabic Vocabulary is practically linear and has a built-in progression, so you'll need to go through the units in order. Importantly, you'll need to try and remember every new word or expression you've learned because it could, and probably will, appear again later. I dare say you'll find it fun and want to go back to the beginning once you've reached the end. But, maybe all authors think that about their book.

There are some practical issues we should point out:

◆ Verbs are presented separately in a list called "It's action time" that covers the past and present tenses.
◆ Vowelling marks are used as necessary in the initial vocabulary lists to clarify pronunciation. In the exercises, the vowelling is sometimes dropped depending on a) how basic the word is and b) how often you have seen the word before. In this way you will train yourself to read Arabic as it is generally presented to adult native speakers, i.e., without any additional vowels.
◆ All the answers to the exercises are at the end.

We hope you enjoy this book while you enrich your vocabulary and get a taste of the light-hearted side of learning Arabic.

Home and town

الجُزْء الأَوَّل: البَيت والمَدينة

The building البِناية

house	بَيت/بُيوت
apartment	شَقّة/شُقَق
entrance	مَدخَل/مَداخِل
stairs	سُلَّم/سَلالِم
elevator	مِصعَد/مَصاعِد
room	غُرفة/غُرَف
bedroom	غُرفة النَّوم/غُرَف النَّوم
sitting room	غُرفة الجُلوس/غُرَف الجُلوس
dining room	غُرفة الطَّعام/غُرَف الطَّعام
hall	صَالة/صَالات
kitchen	مَطبَخ/مَطابِخ
bathroom	حَمّام/حَمّامات
balcony	شُرفة/شُرفات
window	شُبّاك/شَبابيك
door	باب/أَبواب
ceiling	سَقف/أَسقُف
wall	جِدار/جُدران
internal	داخِليّ
external	خارِجيّ
roof	سَطح/أَسطُح
chimney	مَدخَنة/مَداخِن
drain	بَلّاعة/بَلّاعات
garden	حَديقة/حَدائِق

Local flavors

There's another word for wall حائِط/حَوائِط. This is the word used for the Wailing Wall in Jerusalem (حائِط المَبكى). Bethlehem literally means "House of meat" بَيت لَحم.

Traditional Arab houses have an internal courtyard, sometimes with a fountain:

courtyard	باحة/باحات
fountain	نافورة/نافورات

EXERCISE 1·1

Select the English sentence that conveys the meaning of the Arabic.

١ هَل نادية في الشُّرفة؟

Is Nadia in the kitchen?

Is Nadia with you?

Is Nadia on the balcony?

٢ هل الشَّقّة في هذه البِناية؟

Is the apartment in this building?

Are all the stairs in this building?

Is the ceiling in this room?

٣ كُلّ الشَّبابيك في غُرفة واحدة.

All the doors are in the other room.

All the rooms overlook the courtyard.

All the windows are in one room.

٤ غُرفة النَّوم فيها شُبّاك وغُرفة الجُلوس فيها شُرفة.

The window in the kitchen is closed but the door is open.

The bedroom ceiling is high and the balcony is not closed.

The bedroom has a window and the sitting room has a balcony.

٥ باب المِصعَد في مَدخَل البِناية.

The elevator is next to our front door.

The elevator door is at the entrance of the building.

This door leads to the kitchen and bathroom.

٦ الجِدار الخارجيّ بين المَدخَل والحَديقة.

This external wall is between the garden and the kitchen.

The building has an entrance, a garden, and a courtyard.

The external wall is between the entrance and the garden.

It's action time

to rent	اِستَأجَر/يَستَأجِر
to buy	اِشتَرى/يَشتَري
to build	بَنَى/يَبني
to modernize	جَدَّد/يُجَدد
to repair	أصلَح/يُصلِح
to restore	رَمَّم/يُرَمِّم
to demolish	هَدَم/يَهدِم
to paint	دَهَن/يَدهِن
to use	اِستَخدَم/يَستَخدِم
to overlook (e.g. a view)	أَطَلّ (على)/يُطِلّ (على)
to clear (the drains)	سَلَّك/يُسَلِّك (البالوعات)

Handy extras

a place for summer vacations	مَصيف
a place suitable for winter months	مَشتىً
swimming pool	حَمَّام سِباحَة

EXERCISE 1·2

Circle the appropriate word from the list, and then write it in the space provided.

١ اِستَأجَرتُ _____ فيها ٣ غُرَف نَوم مع مَطبخ وحَمّام. (شَقّة/شُبّاك/شُرفَة)

٢ المَبنَى فيه مِصعَد، ولكن أنا استَخدَمتُ _____ (السَّلالِم/البالوعات/الحَوائِط)

٣ غُرفة نوم أحمَد _____ على الحديقة. (تُطِلّ/مَشتىً/تَدهِن)

٤ إنَّهُم _____ البنايات القَديمة. (مَصيف/يُرَمِّمون/يُسَلِّكون)

٥ حَمّام السِّباحَة في _____ (المَطبَخ/الجِدار/الحَديقة)

٦ إنَّه يَبني غُرفة فَوق _____ . (المِصعَد/السَّطح/الباب)

Inside the home داخِل البيت

furniture	أثاث
bed	سَرير/أَسِرَّة
cupboard	خِزانة/خِزانات
table	مائِدة/مَوائِد
chair	كُرسيّ/كَراسيّ
rocking chair	كُرسيّ هَزّاز/كَراسيّ هَزّازة
sofa	أَريكة/أَرائِك
drawer	دُرج/أَدراج
shelf	رَفّ/رُفوف
blanket	بَطّانيّة/بَطّانيّات
carpet	بِساط/أَبسِطة
curtain	سِتار/سَتائِر
mirror	مِرآة/مَرايا
doorbell	جَرَس الباب/أَجراس الأبواب

Water and electricity الماء والكَهرَباء

pipe	ماسُورة/مَواسير
faucet	صُنبور/صَنابير
stopcock	مِحبَس/مَحابِس
hose	خُرطوم/خَراطيم
current	تَيّار/تَيّارات
wire	سِلك/أَسلاك
fan	مَروَحة/مَراوِح
heater; fireplace	مِدفَأة/مَدافِئ
washing machine	غَسّالة/غَسّالات
dishwasher	غَسّالة أَطباق/غَسّالات أَطباق
refrigerator	ثَلّاجة/ثَلّاجات
oven	فُرن/أَفران
blender	خَلّاط/خَلّاطات
iron	مِكواة/مَكاوي
vacuum cleaner	مِكنَسة كهربائية/مَكانِس كهربائية
bucket	جَردَل/جَرادِل
broom	مِقَشّة/مِقَشّات

Local flavors

prayer rug	سَجّادة الصَّلاة
wooden latticework screen	مَشرَبيّة

EXERCISE

1·3

You have a new house, and deliveries are coming in three items at a time as shown by the top lines. Choose where these items should go by circling the correct destination from the bottom line, then write it down in the space provided.

١ غَسّالة أطباق وفُرن وثَلّاجة:

_____ المطبخ/السطح/غرفة النوم

٢ بلّاعة ومِرآة وصُنبور:

_____ الثلاجَة/الحَمّام/المِدفأَة

٣ مِدفأَة ومَروحة وأَريكة:

_____ السطح/الجَردَل/غُرفة الجُلوس

٤ خَلّاط ومقشّة ومائِدة:

_____ الحَمّام/البلّاعة/المطبخ

٥ سِتار وماسورة ومِحبَس:

_____ غُرفة النَّوم/غُرفة الجُلوس/الحَمّام

٦ خِزانة وبَطّانيّة وسَرير:

_____ الفُرن/المِدفأَة/غُرفة النَّوم

EXERCISE

1·4

Circle the object that should not be there.

١ غرفة النوم: بلّاعة/سرير/بطّانيّة

٢ غرفة الجلوس: تلفزيون/أَريكة/جردل

٣ غرفة الطعام: صُنبور/مائدة/كراسيّ

٤ الصالة: مدفأَة/بساط/مقشّة

٥ الحَمّام: ماسورة/مكواة/مِحبَس

٦ المطبخ: غسّالة أطباق/حمّام/ثلّاجة

٧ الشرفة: كراسيّ/مرآة/مائدة

٨ المدخل: سلالم/غرفة طعام/مصعد

٩ الحديقة: خلّاط/خُرطوم/حمّام سباحة

١٠ السطح: مدخل/غرفة/صنبور

١١ المصعد: مرآة/غسّالة/باب

١٢ حمّام السباحة: مَواسير/مصعد/كراسيّ

Around town حَول المَدينة

town/city	مَدينة/مُدُن
capital city	عاصمة/عَواصِم
district/neighborhood	حَيّ/أَحياء
up-scale neighborhood	حَيّ راقٍ/أَحياء راقية
popular neighborhood	حَيّ شَعبيّ/أَحياء شَعبيّة
suburb	ضاحية/ضَواحٍ
slums	عَشوائيّات
edge (of town)	طَرَف/أَطراف (المَدينة)
playground	مَلعَب/مَلاعِب
fence	سور/أَسوار
warehouse	مَخزَن/مَخازِن
factory	مَصنَع/مَصانِع
shopping center	مَركَز التَّسَوُّق/مَراكِز التَّسَوُّق
print shop	مَطبَعة/مَطابِع
observatory	مَرصَد/مَراصِد
cemetery	مَدفَن/مَدافِن
tannery	مَدبَغة/مَدابِغ
auction hall	قاعة مَزادات
statue	تِمثال/تَماثيل
hospital	مُستَشفى/مُستَشفيات
orphanage	مَلجَأ أَيتام/مَلاجئ أَيتام
mill	طاحونة/طَواحين
lighthouse	فَنارة/فَنارات
dam	سَدّ/سُدود
bridge	جِسر/جُسور
train station	مَحَطّة القِطار
platform	رَصيف
quay	رَصيف الميناء

Mr. Anwar, the mayor, is running for re-election in his hometown. Match his achievements as described by his campaign manager.

He repaired the dam.	١ هَدَمَ العَشوائيّات.
He painted the bridges.	٢ رَمَّمَ المَصانِع.
He built the swimming pool.	٣ جَدَّدَ المَلاعِب.
He restored the factories.	٤ أصلَحَ السَّد.
He demolished the slums.	٥ بَنَى حمّام السباحة.
He modernized the playgrounds.	٦ دَهَنَ الجُسور.

Ms. Gihan is also running. Select the matching promises as described by her campaign manager.

She will paint the statues. ١

سَتَدهِن الرَّصيف.

سَتَبني التَّماثيل.

سَتدهِن التَّماثيل.

She will modernize the shopping center. ٢

سَتُجَدِّد مَركَز التَّسَوُّق.

سَتَبني مَركَز التَّسَوُّق.

سَتُجَدِّد المَصانِع والجُسور.

She will repair the playgrounds. ٣

سَتُجَدِّد المَلاعِب.

سَتُصلِح المَلاعِب.

سَتَعبُر المَلاعِب.

She will restore the lighthouse and the windmill. ٤

سَتُرَمِّم التَّماثيل والفَنارة.

سَتُجَدِّد المَصانِع والطاحونة القديمة.

سَتُرَمِّم الفَنارة والطاحونة.

She will build a hospital. ٥

سَتَبني المستشفى.

سَتُجَدِّد المستشفى.

سَتَبني حديقة للأطفال.

She will buy a new telescope for the observatory. ٦

سَتُجَدِّد تليسكوب المَرصَد الجديد.

سَتَشتَري الميكروسكوب الجديد للمُستَشفَى.

سَتَشتَري التليسكوب الجديد للمَرصَد.

Local flavors

mosque	مَسجِد/مَساجِد
minaret	مِئذَنة/مَآذِن
dome	قُبّة/قِباب
(Coptic) church	كَنيسة (قبطيّة)/كَنائِس (قبطيّة)
synagogue	مَعبَد يَهوديّ/مَعابِد يَهوديّة
monument	أثَر/آثار
pyramid	هَرَم/أهرامات
sarcophagus	تابوت/تَوابيت
tomb	ضَريح/أضرِحة
obelisk	مِسَلّة/مِسَلّات
corner	زاوية/زَوايا

The word for "corner" is also used for a simple, out-of-the-way area where Muslims can pray.

Handy extras

Where is "Accident and Emergency"?	أَين قِسم الحَوادِث والطَّوارِئ؟
They use public transport every day.	إنَّهُم يَستَخدِمون المُواصَلات العامّة كُلَّ يَوم.
Suzanne found it in the trash can.	وَجَدَتْهُ سوزان في سَلّة المُهمَلات.
We pay the costs of these public utilities.	نَدفَع تَكاليف هذه المَرافِق العامّة.
I heard that this house is haunted and cursed!	سَمِعتُ أن هذا البَيت مَسكون ومَلعون!
The boy put it in the mailbox.	وَضَعَهُ الوَلَد في صُندوق البَريد.

On the road عَلى الطَّريق

street	شارِع/شَوارِع
road	طَريق/طُرُق
alley	زُقاق/أَزِقَّة
one way	اتِّجاه واحِد
sidewalk	رَصيف الشارِع
footpath	مِدَقّ/مِدَقّات
crossing	مَعبَر/مَعابِر
bend	مُنحَنى/مُنحَنيات
tunnel	نَفَق/أَنفاق
signal	إشارة/إشارات
car	سَيّارة/سَيّارات
truck	شاحِنة/شاحِنات
bicycle	دَرّاجة/دَرّاجات
train	قِطار/قِطارات
bus	باص/باصات
model	طِراز/طُرُز
engine	مُحَرِّك/مُحَرِّكات
tyre	إطار/إطارات
fender	رَفرَف/رَفارِف
load capacity	حُمولة/حُمولات
pedestrians	مُشاة
rush hour	ساعة الذُّروة
convoy	قافِلة/قَوافِل

EXERCISE 1·7

Join the following to create a logical sentence.

على الرصيف.	١ هُناك سيّارات وشاحِنات كثيرة في الطريق
تَماثيل قديمة.	٢ قِسم الحَوادِث والطَّوارِئ
الحديقة والمَلاعِب.	٣ السيّارات في الطريق ولكن المُشاة
في ساعة الذُّروة.	٤ تَستَخدِم سوزان القِطار لأن بيتها في
أطراف المدينة.	٥ أنا في قاعة المَزادات لأنّني أُريد
في المستشفى.	٦ الأولاد في ملجأ الأيتام يُحِبّون

It's action time

to pave	رَصَف/يَرصُف
to plan	خَطَّط/يُخَطِّط
to head (toward)	اتَّجَه/يَتَّجِه
to drive	قاد/يَقود
to cross	عَبَر/يَعبُر
to speed	أسرَع/يُسرِع
to avoid	تَجَنَّب/يَتَجَنَّب

Turn left before the railway crossing.	اتَّجِه إلى اليَسار قَبل المَزلَقان.
You will find the school after the bridge on the right.	سَتَجِد المدرسة بعد الجِسر على اليَمين.
Avoid the airport road.	تَجَنَّبوا طَريق المَطار.
There is a quicker way.	هناك طريقة أسرَع.
We were on our way there.	كُنّا في طَريقنا إلى هُناك.
Can we walk to these stores?	هل نَستَطيع أن نَمشي إلى هذه المَحَلّات؟

EXERCISE 1·8

Of the three Arabic pairs of options, only one pair is reasonably expected to be at the location specified in English. Decide which one.

١ in the apartment

المُنحَنيات والجِسر

الشبّاك والشرفة

الميناء والشاحنات

٢ by the front door

السلّم والجرس

المَزلَقان والقطار

القَوافِل والأنفاق

٣ by the sea

المُحَرّك والبالوعة

الفنارة والميناء

السقف والإطار

on the sidewalk ٤

المطبخ والحمّام

الشاحنات والأريكة

المُشاة والإشارات

by the bed ٥

سَلّة المُهمَلات والمَدفَن

المَدبَغة وقاعة المزادات

المرآة والكرسيّ

by the river ٦

الجسر والسدّ

الباب والرفرف

الدرّاجة والمِدفأَة

Local businesses الأَعمال المَحَلِيّة

store	مَحَلّ/مَحَلّات
bakery	مَخبَز/مَخابِز
butcher	جَزّار/جَزّارون
barber	حَلاق/حَلاقون
jeweler	جَوهَرجيّ/جَوهَرجيّون
restaurant	مَطعَم/مَطاعِم
post office	مَكتَب البَريد/مَكاتب البَريد
laundry	مَغسَلة/مَغاسِل
flower shop	مَحَلّ زُهور/مَحَلّات زُهور
greengrocer	خُضَريّ/خُضَريّون
grocer	بَقّالة/بَقّالات
accounting firm	مَكتَب مُحاسَبة
law practice	مَكتَب مُحاماة
fishmonger	سَمّاك/سَمّاكون
pharmacy	صَيدَليّة/صَيدَليّات
casino	نادي القِمار/نَوادي القِمار
bank	مَصرِف/مَصارِف

Local flavors

spice shop   عَطّار/عَطّارون

kebab man   كَبابجيّ

EXERCISE 1·9

Help me select the logical place to go. Circle the right destination.

١ . . . I'm hungry. I'll go to

الصَّيدَليّة

مَحلّ الزهور

الكَبابجيّ

٢ . . . My hair's too long. I'll go to

السَّمّاك

أطراف المَدينَة

الحَلّاق

٣ . . . It's my mother's birthday. I'll go to

نادي القِمار

بيت أمّي

رَصيف الميناء

٤ . . . I need a new car. I'll go to

مكتب البريد

مَحلّ السيّارات

الجِسر القديم

٥ . . . I'm planning to buy an apartment. I'll go to

المُواصلات العامّة

العَطّار

المَصرِف

٦ . . . I'm flying to New York. I'll go to

المطار

مَحلّ الزهور

مَحلّ البِقالة

Link each phrase with its opposite.

يهدم بيتي	١ بيتي جديد
داخل بيتي	٢ على يمين بيتي
بيتي كبير	٣ خارج بيتي
بعد بيتي	٤ يبني بيتي
بيتي قديم	٥ بيتي صغير
على يسار بيتي	٦ قبل بيتي

Family and friends
الجُزء الثاني: العائِلة والأَصدِقاء

Relatives الأَقارِب

Relatives and families are usually a rich source of strength, solidarity, and supportive affection. However, not all families are blessed with harmony and unity. They are also capable of providing divisiveness, embarrassment, and long-lasting feuds.

relative	قَريب / أَقارِب
family	أُسرة / أُسَر
extended family	عائِلة / عائِلات
father	أَب (أَبو) / آباء
mother	أُمّ / أُمَّهات
brother	أَخ (أَخو) / إخوة
sister	أُخت / أَخَوات
twins	تَوأَم / تَوائِم
son	اِبن / أَبناء
daughter	اِبنة / بَنات
uncle, *maternal*	خال / أَخوال
aunt, *maternal*	خالة / خالات
uncle, *paternal*	عَمّ / أَعمام
aunt, *paternal*	عَمّة / عَمّات
husband	زَوج / أَزواج
wife	زَوجة / زَوجات
children	أَولاد
grandchild	حَفيد / أَحفاد
grandfather	جَدّ / أَجداد
grandmother	جَدّة / جَدّات
father-in-law	حَم (حمو) / أَحماء

mother-in-law	حَماة/حَمَوات
stepbrother	أخ غَير شَقيق
stepsister	أخت غَير شَقيقة
stepfather	زَوج الأُمّ
stepmother	زَوجة الأبّ
distant relative	قَريب من بَعيد

Handy extras

motherhood	أمومة
fatherly kindness	عَطف أَبَوِيّ
brotherly love	حُبّ أَخَوِيّ
Mothers' Day	عيد الأُمّ
the deceased	المَرحوم
family matter	مَوضوع عائِلِيّ

The word مَوضوع is flexible and can be used for:

matter (This is a private matter.)	هذا موضوع خاصّ
issue (This is a sensitive issue.)	هذا موضوع حَسّاس
subject (This is the subject of my letter.)	هذا موضوع خِطابي

EXERCISE 2·1

Select the appropriate word and write it down in the space provided.

١ أبي هو _____ أمّي. (موضوع/زوج/أخت)

٢ جدّتي هي _____ أمّي. (زوجة/حَماة/أمّ)

٣ أنا _____ جدّي. (حفيد/أخت/خال)

٤ أخت أمّي هي _____ (عمّتي/خالي/خالتي)

٥ أمّ زوجتي هي _____ (أمّي/حماتي/جدّتي)

٦ أخو أبي هو _____ (زوجتي/جدّي/عمّي)

٧ هذه الزهور لأمّي. اليوم _____ (موضوع خِطابي/عيد الأمّ/زوجي)

Select the appropriate English sentence.

١ أَذهَب إلى بيت جدّي بالمُواصَلات العامّة.

I went to my grandmother's garden by car today.

Let's go to my aunt's shop. We can take the train.

I go to my grandfather's house by public transport.

٢ زوجي في المَصرِف وابنتي في السينما.

Her father works in a bank beside the cinema.

Our mother was at the cinema but she is out now.

My husband is in the bank and my daughter is in the cinema.

٣ ذَهَبَت جدّتي إلى نادي القِمار في عيد ميلادها.

I went to my grandfather's house on his birthday.

My grandmother went to the casino on her birthday.

Our parents went to the flower shop yesterday.

٤ شقّة خالتي فوق شقّتنا.

Our apartment is above your father's bakery.

Your maternal aunt and my grandmother live here.

Our maternal aunt's apartment is above ours.

٥ أبي وأمّي وأخي وأختي في الشرفة.

My father, mother, brother, and sister are on the balcony.

My father, mother, uncle, and aunt are on the balcony.

I saw your mother, brother, and sister by the mailbox.

٦ سَتَبني حماته لَهُم هذا السور الجديد.

His father-in-law will rent this new house for them.

His mother-in-law will build two new fences for him.

His mother-in-law will build this new fence for them.

People's features مَلامِح النّاس
The head الرَّأس

head	رَأس/رُؤوس
hair	شَعر
forehead	جَبين/أجبِنة
eye	عَين/عُيون
eyelid	جَفن/جُفون
eyebrow	حاجِب/حَواجِب
eyelashes	رِمش/رُموش
nose	أنف/أُنوف
ear	أُذُن/آذان
mouth	فَم/أفواه
lip	شَفة/شِفاه
smile	اِبتِسامة/اِبتِسامات
jaw	فَكّ/فُكوك
teeth	سِنّة/أَسنان
chin	ذَقن/ذُقون
neck	رَقَبة/رِقاب
wrinkles	تَجاعيد
bald patch	صَلعة

Most languages have a *singular* form to describe one common noun (boy, girl, dog, etc.), and a *plural* form to describe two or more common nouns (boys, girls, dogs, etc.). Arabic has a third form especially for two common nouns called the *dual*. So if you were talking about facial features, for example, you would use it for eyes, ears, and eyebrows:

one eye, ear, eyebrow	عَين، أُذُن، حاجِب
two eyes, ears, eyebrows	عَينان، أُذنان، حاجِبان
many eyes, ears, eyebrows	عُيون، آذان، حواجِب

Handy extras

Eastern features	مَلامِح شَرقيّة
curly hair	شَعر مُجَعَّد
dyed hair	شَعر مَصبوغ
blonde (masc., fem.)	أَشقَر، شَقراء
thick eyebrows	حَواجِب كَثيفة

thin mustache	شارِب رَفيع
tattoo	وَشم/وُشوم
gray beard	لِحية بَيضاء

Note that in Arabic hair turns **white** with age, not gray. (More about colors later.)

Local flavors

From my eye! (I will gladly do this for you!)	مِن عيني!
My neck is for you! (I will do anything for you!)	رَقَبتي لَك!
From the sweat of my forehead! (It is legitimately mine!)	مِن عَرَق جَبيني!

EXERCISE

2·3

Circle the appropriate word. Your choice will depend on how many of each feature a normal person is expected to have (one/two/a large number). Then write your answers in Arabic in the space provided.

١ أَنف (واحد/اثنان/عَدَد كبير) _____

٢ جَبين (واحد/اثنان/عَدَد كبير) _____

٣ أُذُن (واحد/اثنان/عَدَد كبير) _____

٤ عَين (واحد/اثنان/عَدَد كبير) _____

٥ رَقَبة (واحد/اثنان/عَدَد كبير) _____

٦ لِحية (واحد/اثنان/عَدَد كبير) _____

٧ وَجه (واحد/اثنان/عَدَد كبير) _____

٨ جَفن (واحد/اثنان/عَدَد كبير) _____

٩ رَأس (واحد/اثنان/عَدَد كبير) _____

١٠ سِنّة (واحد/اثنان/عَدَد كبير) _____

١١ حاجِب (واحد/اثنان/عَدَد كبير) _____

١٢ ذَقن (واحد/اثنان/عَدَد كبير) _____

١٣ رِمش (واحد/اثنان/عَدَد كبير) _____

١٤ شارِب (واحد/اثنان/عَدَد كبير) _____

١٥ فَكّ (واحد/اثنان/عَدَد كبير) _____

The body الجِسم

male	ذَكَر/ نُكور
female	أُنثَى/ إناث
masculinity	ذُكورة
femininity	أُنوثة
youth	شاب/ شَباب
tall	طَويل/ طِوال
short	قَصير/ قِصار
(of) average height	مُتَوَسِّط الطول
dark complexion	بَشرة داكِنة
overweight	بَدين/ بُدُن
thin	نَحيف/ نِحاف
broad-shouldered	عَريض الكَتِفَين
muscular	مَفتول العَضَلات
graceful	رَشيق/ رَشيقون

Character الشَّخصيّة

honest	أَمين/ أُمَناء
attractive	جَذّاب/ جَذّابون
stingy	بَخيل/ بُخَلاء
generous	كَريم/ كُرَماء
poor	فَقير/ فُقَراء
wealthy	ثَرِيّ/ أَثرِياء
greedy	جَشِع/ جَشِعون
careless	مُهمِل/ مُهمِلون
courageous	شُجاع/ شُجعان
belligerent	عُدواني/ عُدوانيون
nosy	فُضوليّ/ فُضوليّون
kind-hearted	طَيِّب القَلب
short-tempered	سَريع الغَضَب
likable, easy to get along with ("digestable")	مَهضوم

Here are two ads from the "Lonely Hearts" section. Read them and then answer the questions that follow. First, this is an ad placed by Gigi Mustafa:

أنا أَبحَث عن شابّ، طويل وعريض الكَتِفَين ومَفتول العَضَلات. بَشرتهُ داكِنة ومَلامحهُ شرقيّة. له شارِب ولِحية. مِن عائلة كبيرة. ثَرِيّ وكريم وجذّاب. عنده سيّارة مِن طِراز جديد وبيت كبير في حيّ راقٍ فيه حديقة وحمّام سباحة. عنده مَصرِف أو مَحَلّ جَوهرجي.

Now, the ad placed by Ali Nasri:

أنا أَبحَث عن شابّة، مُتَوَسِّطة الطول وشَقراء، رَشيقة وأَمينة وتَبتَسِم كثيراً. تحبّ الأطفال والزهور. أنا أَعمَل في مَكتَب مُحاماة صغير. أنا أَستَخدِم المُواصَلات العامّة كلّ يوم ولكن عندي درّاجة وشقّة صغيرة مِن غُرفة واحدة في حيّ شَعبيّ في أطراف المدينة.

EXERCISE
2·4

Decide which translation best represents the Arabic.

١ أنا أبحث عن شابّ طويل.

I am searching for a tall young man.

I have been searching for a long time.

I am searching for a long-term friendship.

٢ هذا الشابّ مفتول العضلات وبشرته داكنة.

I'm hoping to find the right young man for me.

This young man is muscular with a dark complexion.

I can see you are muscular, but you have a dark side.

٣ هذا الشابّ عريض الكتفين وملامحه شرقيّة.

My broad shoulders are one of my better features.

Your shoulders are broad which is an Eastern feature.

This young man has broad shoulders and Eastern features.

٤ هل عندك بيت كبير في حيّ راقٍ؟

Did you buy a big house in this neighborhood?

Do you have a swimming pool in your garden?

Do you have a big house in an up-scale neighborhood?

٥ هل عندك مصرف أو محلّ جوهرجي؟

Does your family own a bank in town?

Do you own a bank or a jewelry store?

Does this bank own a jewelry store?

٦ أنا أبحث عن شابّة شقراء.

I am a blonde young man.

I am looking for a young blonde woman.

A blonde young woman is looking for me.

٧ هذه الشابّة رشيقة وتحبّ الأطفال والزهور.

This young woman is graceful and she loves children and flowers.

These flowers are as beautiful as this young woman over there.

These flowers are so beautiful; they remind me of you.

٨ هل عندك شقّة صغيرة من غرفة واحدة؟

Can I rent an apartment like yours for one year?

Do you have a small one-room apartment?

Do you have one small apartment?

EXERCISE
2·5

Based on the ads, decide whether the statements are true or false.

1. Gigi thinks Ali is just what she's looking for. (T/F)

2. Ali works in a small law firm. (T/F)

3. Gigi doesn't care too much about material things. (T/F)

4. Ali drives to work every morning. (T/F)

5. Gigi appears to like men with beards. (T/F)

6. Ali's apartment is in the city center. (T/F)

Local flavors

hijab (veil covering a woman's hair)	حِجاب/أَحجِبة
A woman wearing a hijab	اِمرأَة مُحَجَّبة
niqab (veil covering a woman's face and hair)	نِقاب
A young woman wearing a niqab	فَتاة مُنَقَّبة
burka (veil covering a woman's whole body, except the eyes)	بُرقُع/بَراقِع
ghutra and *shimaagh* (traditional head covers worn by men, mostly in the Gulf region)	غُطرة وشِماغ

Note how the root is the same for "eyebrow" and "hijab"; it is the root for conceal, protect, or hide.

حَجَب/يَحجُب

Handy extras

Here are a couple of examples of physical features being borrowed to make verbs:

to head (be at the forefront)	تَرَأَّس/يَتَرَأَّس
Who will head the meeting?	مَن سَيَتَرَأَّس الاِجتِماع؟
to tail (to be at the tail end)	تَذَيَّل/يَتَذَيَّل
My name is at the tail end of the guest list!	اِسمي يَتَذَيَّل قائِمة الضُّيوف!

It's action time

to attract	جَذَب/يَجذِب
to repel	نَفَّر/يُنَفِّر
to want	أَراد/يُريد
to love / like	أَحَبَّ/يُحِبّ
to hate	كَرِه/يَكرَه
to behave	تَصَرَّف/يَتَصَرَّف
to sweat	عَرِق/يَعرَق
to pant	لَهَث/يَلهَث

Your friend Dave, who doesn't speak a word of Arabic, has witnessed a robbery in rural Cairo. He is keen on helping the local police by giving them a full description of the criminal. However, there is a major language barrier. You step in and offer to be the police interpreter. Tick the correct translation.

He is a tall man. ١

هو رجل فُضوليّ.

هو رجل طويل.

هو رجل جذّاب.

He has a thick moustache. ٢

له بُرقُع رماديّ.

له لِحية قصيرة.

له شارِب كثيف.

He has short, curly hair and a long beard. ٣

له شعر قصير جذّاب ولحية قصيرة.

له رأس كبير أبيض وشارب صغير.

له شعر قصير مُجَعَّد ولحية طويلة.

His nose is big. ٤

أنفهُ كبير.

أنفهُ جذّاب.

أنفهُ أبيض.

He was sweating a lot. ٥

كان يَعرَق كثيراً.

كان فُضوليّا جداً.

كان يَحجِب كلَّ شيء.

He has an honest face and an attractive smile. ٦

له رأس كبير وشعر جذّاب.

له وَجه أمين وابتسامة جذّابة.

له ابتسامة جذّابة وذَقنهُ كبير.

Select the Arabic expression that best describes the following characters and their behavior.

١ He sails around the world in two luxury yachts, one for him, and one for his staff.

رجل جذّاب/رجل فُضوليّ/رجل ثريّ

٢ She opened and looked inside every drawer, box, bag, jar, and envelope in our house.

إمرأة مُحَجَّبة/إمرأة فُضوليّة/إمرأة جذّابة

٣ He sat down, then ordered every dish on the menu.

رجل له شارب كثيف/رجل له لحية طويلة/رجل جَشِع

٤ The bride stood on a chair to kiss the groom on the cheek.

فتاة مُنَقَّبة/فتاة قصيرة/فتاة مَلامِحها شَرقيّة

٥ Last summer we worked in his garden for 6 hours and he didn't even offer us a glass of water.

رجل بَخيل/رجل له لحية بَيضاء/رجل له ابتسامة جذّابة

٦ She returned the gold watch I had forgotten in her taxi.

إمرأة شعرها قصير/فتاة أمينة/فتاة أنفها كبير

It's action time

to be born	وُلِد/يولَد
to die	مات/يَموت
to ask (a question, mostly)	سَأَل/يَسأَل
to ask (a favor, mostly)	طَلَب/يَطلُب
to marry	تَزَوَّج/يَتَزَوَّج
to accept	وافَق/يُوافِق
to decline	رَفَض/يَرفُض
to discuss	ناقَش/يُناقِش
to chatter	ثَرثَر/يُثَرثِر

In each group, there are two people who have similar views or habits, and one who differs.
See if you can spot the one who differs.

١ تُحِبّ زوجة عَمّي أن تُثَرِثر.

تُثَرثِر سميرة كثيراً مع أمّي.

لا تُثَرثِر عَمّتي مع أبي.

٢ قال أبي "لا!".

وافَقَت خالتي.

رَفَضَت عَمّتي.

٣ أعمامي كُلّهُم أثرِياء وكُرَماء.

كلّ عائلتي فُقَراء وبُخَلاء.

خالتي كَريمة وثَرية.

٤ أنا لا أُريد أن أَتَزَوّج أَبَداً.

وافَقَت داليا لأنّها تُريد أن تَتَزَوّج أحمد.

تَرفُض سميرة اِبنة خالتي الزَّواج تَماماً.

٥ وافَقَت أمّي وقالَت: رَقَبَتي لك!

اِبتَسمَ أبي وقال: من عيني!

رَفَضَت عَمّتي وقالَت: لا تُناقِشني!

٦ أنا لا أُحِبّ الشَّوارِب.

تَكرَه جيهان الشَّوارِب.

تُحِبّ سميرة شارِب زَوجها.

Local flavors

الوَلَد لِـخاله

the boy (takes after) his maternal uncle

Arab family members will look for similarities between a young son and his maternal uncle to show how true this expression is. Chances are, if you look hard enough you will find something in common between them.

In English, many things can sometimes be described as heavy: "a heavy load," "heavy industry," and even "a heavy heart."

In Arabic, you can add "heavy shadow"; we say "heavy-shadowed" to suggest someone is totally humorless:

ثَقيل الظِّلّ

And we say "heavy-blooded" to suggest someone is insufferable.

ثَقيل الدَّم

In addition, here are a few more things that can also be "heavy" in Arabic:

hearing: hard of hearing

ثَقيل السَّمع

an annoying guest, perhaps overstaying his or her welcome

ثَقيل ضَيف

In addition, there are two types of men that are described as "heavy":

an attractive young man who pretends to be not interested in girls

شابّ ثَقيل

and an older, richer man with an air of authority about him

رَجُل ثَقيل

As for lightness, we have . . .

lightness of the hand; useful for picking pockets, giving injections, and similar activities

خَفيف اليَد

lightness of movement; agility and nimbleness

خَفيف الحَرَكة

And, lightness of shadow and blood, which are the opposite of what we've described above

خَفيف الظِّلّ وخَفيف الدَّم

Social occasions المُناسَبات الاِجتِماعيّة

party/event	حَفلة / حَفلات
charity event	حَفل خَيريّ / حَفلات خَيريّة
banquet	مَأدُبة / مَآدِب
engagement	خُطوبة / خُطوبات
wedding	حَفل الزَّفاف / حَفلات الزَّفاف
wedding procession	زَفّة / زَفّات
birthday	عيد ميلاد / أعياد ميلاد
circumcision	طُهور
funeral	جَنازة / جَنازات
wake	مَأتم / مَآتم

Handy extras

mother of the bride	أُمّ العَروس
courtesy visit	زِيارة مُجامَلة/زيارات مُجامَلة
greeting the neighbors	تَحِيّة الجيران
religious occasion	مُناسَبة دينيّة/مُناسَبات دينيّة
social activities	اِجتِماعيّات

Local flavors

incense	بُخور
sherbet	شَربات

Traditionally, the first step in the marriage process is that the young man and his father approach the young woman's father to ask for her hand in marriage. If everyone broadly agrees and the man is accepted, the father and future son-in-law shake hands and recite together the first chapter/surat (سُورَة) of the Quran, called the Opener (الفاتحة).

This is followed by a round of sherbet and some high-pitched trilling (زَغاريد) by the women-folk. These alert the neighbors that something really special has just happened in that particular household.

Quite often, the women will have already done all the preliminary testing of the waters before any of this actually happens.

I'm going to have lunch with my fiancee.	سَأَتناوَل الغَداء مع خَطيبَتي.
My mother-in-law likes green tea.	حَماتي تُحِبّ الشاي الأَخْضَر.
His widow is quite young.	أرمَلتهُ صَغيرة السِّن.
triple divorce	طَلاق بالثَّلاثة

Many years ago, a man could divorce his wife, in a moment of madness, by saying "I divorce you!" Mind you, saying "I divorce you!" just *once* meant that the door was left slightly ajar, and they could, technically, kiss and make up. They would be still married, and they could live happily ever after.

But, then again, in a moment of weakness, for example, this whole scenario could be repeated for a *second* time.

However, and it's a big however, if it happened for a *third* time it is final and they cannot remarry unless she marries, then divorces, a different man first.

Write the opposite of each word in the space provided.

١ يَرفُض _____

٢ نَحيف _____

٣ كَريم _____

٤ قَصير _____

٥ يَكرَه _____

٦ زَواج _____

Complete each of the following sentences by making the logical choice from the three options that follow it.

١ أحمد رجل جَذّاب لأنه ...

طويل وخفيف الدم وكريم.

بدين وبخيل وقصير.

جَشِع وبخيل ويَعرَق كثيراً.

٢ تعيش داليا في نعيم لأن ...

زوجها فقير وفُضولي وبدين.

خطيبها ثريّ وكريم ويُحبّها.

حَماتها بخيلة وتُثَرثِر كثيراً معها.

٣ كلّ الجيران يُحِبّون أنور لأنّه ...

يَكرَه الابتسام والتحيّة والحفلات.

ثقيل الظلّ ويُحِبّ المَأتم والجِنازات.

كريم ويُحِبّ الجيران والمُناسَبات الاِجتِماعيّة.

٤ أُحِبّ في أبي ...

أنّه كريم وخفيف الدم.

أنّه بخيل وثقيل الظلّ ويَرفُض الابتسام.

أنّه فُضوليّ وجَشِع ويَكرَه عيد ميلادي.

٥ تَكرَه حماتي ...

الكرم والأمانة والابتسام.

أن تعيش في نعيم.

تَـجاعيد الوَجه.

٦ كلّ أصدقائي يُحبّون أمّي لأنّها ...

بخيلة وفُضوليّة.

مُنَفِّرة وتَرفُض كلّ شيء.

كريمة وتُحِبّ الابتسام.

You are an ace secret agent monitoring a dangerous gang of thieves from the roof of a high building. Your team is spread out everywhere below, and you relay anything suspicious to them using concealed radio. Choose the Arabic sentence that best describes what you are seeing.

١ "On train station platform. Tall man. Thick moustache."

على رصيف الميناء. رجل طويل. ثقيل السَّمع.

على رصيف محطّة القطار. رجل طويل. شارب كثيف.

على رصيف محطّة القطار. رجل قصير. خفيف الحَرَكة.

٢ "Entrance to orphanage. Thin woman. Short hair. Big nose."

مَدخَل المَطبَعة. أَرمَلة صغيرة في السنّ. شعر مُجَعَّد.

سُلَّم قاعة المَزادات. زوجة عمّي. حَواجِب كثيفة.

مَدخَل المَلجَأ. امرأة نحيفة. شعر قصير. أنف كبير.

٣ "Hospital stairs. Short woman. Large tattoo on neck."

سَلالِم المَصنَع. أمّ العَروسة. حماتي تـحبّ الشاي الأخضر.

سَلالِم المُستَشفى. إمرأة قصيرة. وَشم كبير على الرَّقَبة.

سَلالِم المُستَشفى. رجل قصير. تِمثال كبير.

4 "Three now together on sidewalk. They chatter outside jewelry store."

ثلاثة رِجال في مِصعَد. كرسيّ هَزّاز. اِتِّجاه واحد.

الثلاثة الآن بِجانِب فَنارة بيضاء يُثَرثِرون خارج المَصنَع.

الثلاثة الآن مَعاً على رصيف الشارع. يُثَرثِرون خارج محلّ الجَوهرجي.

5 "They enter jewelry store. Three minutes inside."

الثلاثة الآن مع رجل قصير. يَشتَرون ثلاثة كراسيّ.

يَدخُلون محلّ الجَوهرجي. في الداخل ثلاث دَقائِق.

الباب والرُّفرف والأريكة. ثلاثة رِجال في المِصعَد.

6 "Out of jewelry store. Speeding toward car. Car speeding toward tunnel."

خارج البيت المَسكون. يُسرِعون باتِّجاه الأحياء الراقية. هناك سيّارتَين.

يخرجون من محلّ الجَوهرجي. يُسرِعون باتِّجاه سيّارة. تُسرِع السيّارة باتِّجاه النَّفَق.

نَستطيع أن نَمشي إلى هذه المحلّات. ولكن أنا لا أرى. هناك طريقة أَسرَع.

7 "Inside tunnel. Tunnel conceals everything. I'm having lunch now."

ثلاثة كراسي هَزّازة. وَشم كبير على رَقَبته. يُثَرثِرون.

في النَّفَق. يَحجُب النفق كلّ شيء. سَأتناوَل الغداء الآن.

في مِصعَد. يَحجُب الرجل كلّ شيء. يتناوَلون الغداء.

Describing this and that

الجُزءُ الثالِث: وَصف هذا وهذه

Some descriptions   بَعض الأوصاف

broad	عَريض
narrow	ضَيِّق
spacious	فَسيح
weak	ضَعيف
sturdy	مَتين
transparent	شَفّاف
simple	بَسيط
complicated	مُعَقَّد
empty	فارِغ
vertical	عَمُوديّ
horizontal	أُفُقيّ
forward	أَماميّ
backward	خَلفيّ
inverted	مَعكوس
visible	ظاهِر
hidden	خَفِيّ

Shape   شَكل/أَشكال

square	مُرَبَّع/مُرَبَّعات
rectangle	مُستَطيل/مُستَطيلات
triangle	مُثَلَّث/مُثَلَّثات
circle	دائِرَة/دَوائِر
pointed	مُدَبَّب
flat	مُسَطَّح
oval	بَيضاويّ

round	مُستَدير
spherical	كُرَويّ
conical	مَخروطيّ
spiral	حَلَزونيّ
cubic	مُكَعَّب
curve	مُنحَنٍ/مُنحَنيات
diameter	قُطر/أَقطار
radius	نِصف قُطر الدَّائِرَة

Complete each of the following sentences by making the logical choice from the three options that follow it.

١ لا توجد شاحنات كبيرة على الجسر لأنّه ...

ضَعيف وقَديم.

قَصير ومُكَعَّب.

شَفَّاف وأَخضر.

٢ الأولاد يحبّون هذا المَلعَب لأنّه ...

مَسكون ومَلعون.

يَحجُب كلّ شيء.

فَسيح وفارِغ.

٣ سَئَلَ المُدَرِّس الأولاد عن قُطر ...

الكتاب.

الدائرة.

الثَلّاجة.

٤ يحبّ المُشاة هذا الرَّصيف لأنّه ...

عَريض.

خَفيف.

حَلَزونيّ.

٥ تُريد زَوجتي هذه الأريكة لأنّها ...

مَعكوسة.

مَتينة.

على اليمين.

٦ نُريد أثاثنا الآن لأن ...

شقّتنا فارغة.

رَصيف الميناء على اليسار.

مَلامِحنا شَرقيّة.

Handy extras

| There is a massive difference between them. | هناك فَرق شاسِع بَينهما. |
| It covers vast areas. | إنّها تُغَطّي مِساحات شاسِعَة. |

Local flavors

"Has a long tongue": used to describe someone who is rude and insolent.	لِسانُه طَويل
"Has a long hand": prone to stealing	يَدُه طَويلَة
"Has a long arm": prone to hitting others	ذِراعُه طَويل
"Has a long neck": proud	رَقَبَتُه طَويلَة

Other descriptions أوصاف أُخرى

liquid	سائِل/سَوائِل
powder	مَسحوق/مَساحيق
paste	مَعجون/مَعاجين
lump	كُتلَة/كُتَل
heap	كَومة/أكوام
shallow	ضَحل
deep	عَميق
thorny	شائِك
high	مُرتَفِع
low	مُنخَفِض
clear	واضِح

unclear	غامِض
rough	خَشِن
smooth	ناعِم
soft	طَرِيّ
waxy	شَمعِيّ
greasy	دُهني
concentrated	مُرَكَّز
slippery	زَلِق
pure	نَقيّ
polluted	مُلَوَّث
sticky	لَزِج
slight	ضَئيل
giant	عِملاق
covered	مُغَطّى
exposed	مَكشوف

Write the opposite of each word or expression in the space provided.

_____	١ عموديّ
_____	٢ متين
_____	٣ مُعَقَّد
_____	٤ على اليسار
_____	٥ قصير
_____	٦ مُلَوَّث
_____	٧ أماميّ
_____	٨ مُنخَفِض
_____	٩ غامض
_____	١٠ مَكشوف

Handy extras

Note the root: ف/ش/ك ka/sha/fa, to expose/to reveal, can be used to say . . .

He discovered that his car had disappeared.	اِكْتَشَفَ أَنَّ سَيّارتُه اِخْتَفَتْ.
The doctor examined my son.	كَشَفَ الطَّبيب عَلَى ابني.
I will never divulge the secret.	لَن أَكْشِف السِّرّ أبداً.
We'll wait until matters become clearer.	سَنَنْتَظِر حَتّى تَتَكَشَّف الأُمور.
This is an amazing discovery, professor!	هَذا اِكْتِشاف مُذهِل يا بروفيسير!
They are away on a trip with the boy-scouts.	إنّهم في رِحلة مع الكَشّافة.
Is this the final statement of accounts?	هل هذا هو كَشف الحِساب النِّهائيّ؟
We used the searchlights to look for the escaped prisoners.	اِسْتَخْدَمنا الأنوار الكَشّافة في البَحث عَن المَساجين الهاربين.
Your cover has been blown! You are a spy!	اِنكَشَفَ أَمرُك! أَنتَ جاسوس!

EXERCISE

3·3

Circle the appropriate word and then write it down in the space provided.

١ مَلعَب الجودو _____ ولكن ملعب التنس مكشوف. (مُغطّى/بُرتُقاليّ/خَشِن)

٢ الأطفال يحبّون حمّام السباحة _____ . (النِهائيّ/الشائِك/الضَّحل)

٣ أريد مائدة كبيرة و _____ لعائِلتي وضُيوفي. (مُستَديرة/زَلِقة/خَشِنة)

٤ اِنتَظِرْ حَتّى تَتَكَشَّف الأُمور لأنّ هذا موضوع عائِليّ _____ . (مُستَطيل/شائِك/مَخروطيّ)

٥ الغسّالة و _____ في الحمّام على اليمين. (ملعب الجولف/المَسحوق/الشاجِنة)

٦ هذا سِرّ _____ لا أَكْشِفهُ أبداً! (معكوس/عميق/نِصف قُطر الدائرة)

It's action time

to form	شَكَّل/يُشَكِّل
to divide	قَسَّم/يُقَسِّم
to separate	فَصَل/يَفصِل
to bend	لَوى/يَلوي
to grind	طَحَن/يَطحَن
to inflate	نَفَخ/يَنفُخ
to freeze	جَمَّد/يُجَمِّد
to fold	طَوى/يَطوي

More descriptions

necessary	لازِم
rare	نادِر
suitable	مُناسِب
proportionate	مُتَناسِب
relative	نِسبيّ
widespread	مُنتَشِر
movable	مُتَنَقِّل
desirable	مَرغوب
in demand	مَطلوب
contemporary	مُعاصِر
reasonable	مَعقول

Colors الألوان

The six basic colors at the top of the list below have their own feminine form which is included in parentheses.

red	أَحمَر (حَمراء)
green	أَخضَر (خَضراء)
yellow	أَصفَر (صَفْراء)
blue	أَزرَق (زَرقاء)
black	أَسوَد (سَوداء)
white	أَبيَض (بَيْضاء)
brown	بُنّيّ
orange	بُرتُقاليّ
pink	وَرديّ
grey	رَماديّ
purple	بَنَفسَجيّ

Local flavors

kohl-blue (deep)	كُحليّ
olive-colored	زَيتونيّ
honey-colored	عَسَليّ
lime-colored	لَيمونيّ
apricot-colored	مشمِشيّ
sky-blue	أَزرَق سَمائيّ

Select the logical answer and write it in the space provided.

١ اِبنتي تحبّ ـــــــــ (المصنع/محلّ الزهور/المستشفى) لأن فيه ألوان كثيرة.

٢ فيلم السينما القديم كان ـــــــــ (أبيض/عسليّ/أحمر) و ـــــــــ (أخضر/أسود/ليمونيّ).

٣ مَلاعِب الجولف دائماً ـــــــــ (زرقاء/خضراء/سوداء) و ـــــــــ. (مَعقولة/فسيحة/مُتَنَقِّلة)

٤ مَلامِحها شرقيّة. شَعرها ـــــــــ (أخضر/برتقاليّ/أسود) وعُيونها ـــــــــ (بنيّة/مشمشيّة/صَفراء).

٥ ألوان السيّارات كثيرة جدّاً، ولكن الإطارات دائماً ـــــــــ (ليمونيّة/بنفسجيّة/سوداء).

٦ هل تحبّ الزَّيتون (الأزرق والأبيض/الأحمر والكحلي/الأسود والأخضر)؟

How much? كَم؟

quantity	كَميّة/كَميّات
tenth	عُشر / أَعشار
quarter	رُبع / أَرباع
third (one-third)	ثُلث / أَثلاث
half	نِصف / أَنصاف
three quarters	ثلاثة أَرباع
inch	بوصة/بوصات
hand span	شِبر/ أَشبار
foot	قَدَم/ أَقدام
pound	رَطل/ أَرطال
ounce	أُوقية/ أُوقيات
drop	قَطرة/ قَطرات
jugful	مِلْء إبريق
three glasses	ثلاثة أكواب
teaspoon	مِلعَقة شاي/ مَلاعِق شاي
piece	قِطعة/ قِطَع
handful	حَفنة/ حَفنات
sum (of money)	مَبلَغ/ مَبالِغ
wage; fee	أَجر/ أُجور
minimum	الحَدّ الأَدنَى
maximum	الحَدّ الأَقصَى

surplus to requirements	زائِد عن الحاجة
additional quantity	كَمِّية إضافيّة / كَمِّيات إضافيّة
double	الضِّعف
multiples	أضعاف
majority	أَكثَرِيّة / أَكثَرِيّات
minority	أَقَلِّية / أَقَلِّيّات

Here are three ways to say "most people": مُعظَم الناس / أغلَب الناس / أكثَر الناس

Professor Boutros claims he has discovered a revolutionary new fuel for cars. A waiting worldwide audience pants with anticipation as he is being interviewed on television:

Interviewer: "Tell us about your discovery, Professor Boutros!"

بروفيسور بطرس: "يُناسِب اِكتِشافي كلّ سيّارة من أيّ طِراز، و يُناسِب كلّ شاحِنة بأيّ حُمولة على الطريق اليوم. إنّه يناسب كلّ المُحَرِّكات. إنّه اِكتِشاف بسيط جدًّا. أنا اِكتَشَفتُه في مَطبَخي، والآن سيّارتي هي أسرَع سيّارة في المدينة."

Interviewer: "Your kitchen? So are you saying that anyone can easily make this new fuel at home?"

بروفيسور بطرس: "نعم. في أيّ مطبخ أو حمّام."

Interviewer: "Wonderful! So what does one need to make it?"

بروفيسور بطرس: "كيلو من مَعجون المِشمِش الطَّرِيّ، وكيلو من مَسحوق البرتقال الشمعيّ من عند الخُضَريّ، مع نِصف كيلو من لِسان السمك الدُّهنيّ من عند السمّاك. ثلاثة أكواب من عصير الليمون المُرَكَّز مع حَفنة من الشاي الأخضر الناعِم. كيلو من معجون الزيتون الأخضر النَّقِيّ ومِلعَقة شاي من معجون الزيتون الأسود المُرَكَّز."

Interviewer: "Very interesting, Professor."

بروفيسور بطرس: "نعم. ثُمَّ مِلء إبريق من شَربات الزُّهور الأحمر اللَزِج. ومن عند الحلّاق سَنَحتاج إلى ثلاثة أرطال من الشعر الأشقَر الشائك من الشَّوارِب، وكُتلة كبيرة إضافيّة من الشعر الأبيض الخَشِن من اللِّحية، لأن شعر الرأس لا يُناسِب هذا الاِكتِشاف."

Interviewer: "Yes, but . . ."

بروفيسور بطرس: "أنا وَضَعتُ كلّ هذا في الخَلّاط ثُمَّ اِشتَرَيتُ جَردَلًا فارغًا ومتينًا. وضعتُ اكتشافي في الجردل ومعه مِلء إبريق عَميق من معجون الأسنان السائِل وكومة كبيرة من البُخور المَطحون."

Interviewer: "This seems a little complicated, Professor."

بروفيسور بطرس: "هذا مَوضوع نِسبيّ!"

Select the English that best communicates the Arabic.

١ مَعجون المشمش الطريّ

sweet apricot jelly

soft apricot paste

invisible apricot juice

٢ مَسحوق البُرتُقال الشَّمعيّ

fresh orange juice

empty orange jug

waxy orange powder

٣ لِسان السَّمك الدُهنيّ

greasy fish tongue

fishy grease jars

fishy tongue in cheek

٤ عَصير اللَّيمون المُرَكَّز

a hint of lemon zest

concentrated lemon juice

lemon-flavored drinks

٥ الزيتون الأخضَر النَقيّ

olive-colored paste

black and green olives

pure green olives

٦ شَربات الزهور الأحمَر اللَّزِج

red, sticky flower sherbet

flower sherbet with lemon

flowery red and orange pie

٧ هذا موضوع نسبيّ!

This is a relative issue!

It was a sticky subject!

This is a sensitive issue!

Fill in the gaps in the English to match the Arabic.

١ أنا اكتشفتُهُ في مطبخي.

I _____ it in my _____ .

٢ أيّ سيّارة وأيّ شاحنة

any _____ and any _____

٣ إنه يُناسب كلّ المحرّكات.

It _____ all _____ .

٤ وضعتُ كلّ هذا في الخلّاط.

I put _____ of this in the _____ .

٥ هذا الجردل الفارغ متين وشقّاف.

This empty bucket is _____ and _____ .

٦ معجون الأسنان السائل

liquid _____

After the interview, two car enthusiasts were having a debate in which they were on opposite sides. Match the opposites.

محرّك ضَيِّق	١ مُحَرّك بسيط
محرّك ضعيف	٢ محرّك أماميّ
محرّك مُعَقَّد	٣ محرّك خَفيّ
محرّك قديم	٤ محرّك متين
محرّك بِصَوت مُنخَفِض	٥ محرّك مُغَطّى
محرّك خلفيّ	٦ محرّك بالحدّ الأقصى
محرّك بِحَرَكة خَشِنة	٧ محرّك عريض
محرّك ظاهر	٨ محرّك بِصَوت عالٍ
محرّك مكشوف	٩ محرّك مُعاصِر
محرّك بالحدّ الأدنى	١٠ محرّك بِحَرَكة ناعمة

Handy extras

It's a drop in the ocean.	إنّها قَطرة في المُحيط.
We will need to double the production.	سنَحتاج إلى مُضاعَفة الإنتاج.
part (of)	جُزء (من)/ أَجزاء (من)
even (number)	رَقم زَوجيّ/ أَرقام زَوجيّة
odd (number)	رَقم فَرديّ/ أَرقام فَرديّة

Materials المَوادّ

marble	رُخام
metal	مَعدِن/ مَعادِن
cement	إسمَنت
ceramics	خَزَف
scrap iron	حَديد خُردة
bamboo	خَيزران
glass	زُجاج
wood	خَشَب/ أَخشاب
sand	رَمل/ رِمال
steel	صُلب
straw	قَشّ
stone	حَجَر/ أَحجار

EXERCISE 3·8

You are in real estate and have inspected a new luxury villa that's up for sale. These are the quick notes you prepared. Complete the Arabic version of your notes, using the English for reference.

١. Desirable, in-demand suburb. Broad street. White external walls.

ضاحية _____ ومَطلوبة. شارِع _____ . _____ الخارجيّة بيضاء.

٢. Garden has visible character. Lots of flowers.

الحديقة لها شَخصيّة _____ . الكثير من _____ .

٣. Hidden entrance to swimming pool, children's playground, and tennis court.

مَدخَل _____ لحمّام السباحة، و _____ الأطفال والتنس.

٤. Marble stairs. Doors and windows are green. Statues in spacious balconies.

سَلالِم من _____ . الأبواب والشبابيك _____ . تَماثيل في الشُّرفات _____ .

High ceiling. Exposed wood. Fireplace. ٥

_____ مرتفع. الخشب _____. مدفأة.

Massive living room. To be divided? To be separated? ٦

حجرة الجلوس _____. تُقَسَّم؟ _____ ؟

Oval kitchen. Round bathrooms. ٧

مطبخ _____. حمّامات _____ .

Rare. Reasonable sum. I approve. ٨

_____. مبلغ _____. أنا أُوافِق.

EXERCISE 3·9

I have bought lots of stuff for my new hotel. Help me select the logical destination. Circle the right word.

١ أنا أشتريتُ الكثير من الزهور المُلَوَّنة. سَنَضَعها في ...

الصَّيدلية

المَدخَل

الحلّاق

٢ أنا أشتريتُ الكثير من المَوائد المتينة. سَنَضَعها في ...

المطعم

الشارع

السيّارة

٣ أنا أشتريتُ الكثير من الزيتون والمشمش والبرتقال. سَنَضَعها في ...

السُّلَّم

المدفأة

المطبخ

٤ أنا اشتريتُ الكثير من الكراسيّ الخشبيّة. سَنَضَعها في ...

الخلّاط

حمّام السباحة

غرفة حفيدي

٥ أنا اِشتريتُ كميّات إضافيّة من الأثاث. سَنَضَعها في ...

الفُرن

المَدبَغة

المَخزن

٦ أنا أشتريتُ كميّة صغيرة من الكباب لأَتناوَل الغداء. سَنَضَعها في ...

الثَّلّاجة

المِدق

الطاحونة

Seeing there is no future in alternative fuel, Professor Boutros decides to become a marriage councilor. This is a transcript from the tape of his first case, Majid and Hoda:

هدى: يا بروفيسور بُطرُس، نَحن كُنّا نَعيش في نَعيم. حُبّ كبير وزَواج متين، ولكن ماجِد هَدَمَ كلّ شيء.

ماجِد: هُناك فَرق شاسع بَيننا.

هدى: نعم. أنا إمرأَة نادرة. لأنّني مَرغوبة، وشَخصيّتي ناعمة، طريّة، ولكنّها شخصيّة قويّة وعَميقة.

ماجِد: عَميقة؟! يا بروفيسور بُطرُس، رأس زَوجتي مُسَطَّح. سَتَجدها أمام التليفزيون أو المرآة أو تُثَرثِر في التليفون. هذا هو سَقفها!

هدى: ماجِد لِسانهُ طَويل ورأسُه فارغ. زَوجي رجل ضعيف يا بروفيسور.

ماجِد: أنا تَزَوَّجتُها لأنّها كانت رشيقة وجذّابة وكلّها أُنوثة. والآن . . . أنا تَزَوَّجتُ ثَلّاجة يا بروفيسور!

هدى: أنا وافقتُ لأن ماجِد كان يَطلُب منّي الزواج سَبَع مَرّات كلّ يوم! كان يقول لي "رَقَبتي لكِ يا هدى! عَيني لكِ يا هدى!"

ماجِد: كُلّ أَقاربي قالوا لا! لا تَتَزَوَّجها! ولكن أنا تَزَوَّجتُها لأنّها قالَت أَنّها تُحِبّني. الآن فَقَط تَكَشَّفَت الأمور.

هدى: وأنا تَزَوَّجتُه لأن أُمّه قالَت لي أنّه كريم وثريّ جدّاً! والآن اِكتَشَفتُ أنّه بخيل وفقير! بروفيسور بُطرُس: هذه كلّها مواضيع بَسيطة.

Choose the English sentence that best describes the Arabic.

١ أنا إمرأة نادرة ومرغوبة. كُنّا نَعيش في نَعيم.

I am a cultured and sensitive woman. We were living in misery.

He is a lovely man with rare qualities. We must try harder.

I am a rare and desirable woman. We were living in paradise.

٢ زوجي هَدَمَ كلّ شيء. حبّ كبير وزواج متين.

My marriage means everything to me. I will do everything to save it.

My husband demolished everything. A big love and a sturdy marriage.

My husband meant everything to me. But now, everything has changed.

٣ رأسها مُسَطَّح. المرأة والتليفزيون والتليفون هي سَقفها.

Her flat screen television took her away from me. She ignored the telephone.

Her head is flat. The mirror, the television, and the telephone are her ceiling.

I stared at the ceiling as she watched television. That's not a life any more.

٤ أُمّه قالت لي أنّه كريم وثريّ.

His mother told me he was generous and wealthy.

He told me his mother was generous and wealthy.

His mother told me he ate ice cream three times a day.

٥ كانت رشيقة وجذّابة وكلّها أُنوثة.

She was a graceful dancer and a gifted singer.

She was graceful, attractive, and full of feminity.

She was attractive in a feminine sort of way.

٦ هذه كلّها مواضيع بسيطة.

These issues can be dealt with.

These are all simple matters.

I think the solution is simple.

Now decide what is true and what is false:

1. Hoda thinks Majid has destroyed their marriage. (T/F)

2. Majid thinks Hoda has a towering intellect. (T/F)

3. Hoda believes their marriage is solid. (T/F)

4. All of Majid's family were keen on Hoda. (T/F)

5. Majid used to ask Hoda to marry him about seven times a day. (T/F)

6. Majid's mother told Hoda that he was rich and generous. (T/F)

7. Hoda and Majid will live happily ever after. (T/F)

EXERCISE
3·12

Choose the Arabic sentence that best describes the English.

My character is deep, but it is soft and smooth. ١

شخصيّتي ناعِمة، لأنني إمرأة نادرة وعميقة.

أنا إمرأة نادرة لأنني عميقة وأحب زوجي.

شخصيّتي عميقة، ولكنها ناعمة وطريّة.

I am a rare woman, graceful and attractive. ٢

أنا إمرأة جذّابة، رشيقة ونادرة.

أنا إمرأة نادرة، رشيقة وجذّابة.

أنا زوجة ناعمة، شخصيّتي نادرة.

You will find her over there, chatting on the telephone. ٣

التليفون هناك، ستجده بجوار الباب.

زوجتي الناعمة تثرثر في التليفون.

ستجدها هناك، تثرثر في التليفون.

Now, matters have become clearer. ٤

الآن هو أفضل الأوقات.

الآن، تَكَشَّفَت الأمور.

هذا هو الموضوع النادر.

Is he rich and generous, or poor and stingy? ٥

هل هي رشيقة وجذّابة أم فقيرة وبخيلة؟

هل هو ثريّ وكريم أم فقير وبخيل؟

هل هي نادرة وعميقة أم رشيقة وثريّة؟

I will demolish this solid house! ٦

أنا سأبني البيت ثمّ أهدمه!

هذا أفضل البيوت المتينة اليوم!

أنا سأهدم هذا البيت المتين!

Time
الجُزء الرابِع: الوَقت

A special week أُسبوع خاصّ

closed Sunday	مُغلَق يَوم الأَحَد
try on Monday	حاوِل يَوم الاثنَين
next Tuesday	يَوم الثُّلاثاء القادِم
definitely on Wednesday	أَكيد يَوم الأَربِعاء
last Thursday	يَوم الخَميس الماضي
except Fridays	ما عَدا أَيَّام الجُمعة
maybe Saturday evening	رُبَّما مَساء السَّبت

From time to time مِن وَقت إلى آخَر

today	اليَوم
tomorrow	غَداً
yesterday	أَمس
daily	يَوميّ
weekly	أُسبوعيّ
monthly	شَهريّ
yearly	سَنَويّ
next week	الأُسبوع القادِم
last month	الشَّهر الماضي
hourly	كُلّ ساعة
until now	حَتَّى هذه الساعَة
at any hour	في أَيّ ساعة
in an hour	بَعدَ ساعة
within an hour	خِلال ساعة
for two hours	لِمُدّة ساعتَين
five minutes ago	مُنذُ خَمس دَقائِق

once every week	مَرّة كُلّ أُسبوع
twice a year	مَرّتَين في السَّنة

Long time وَقت طَويل

once in a lifetime	مَرّة في العُمر
in the future	في المُستَقبَل
my whole life	حَياتي كُلّها
all my life	طَوال عُمري
forever	إلى الأَبَد
never	أَبَداً
indefinitely	إلى ما لا نِهاية

Local flavors

The month of Ramadan	شَهر رَمَضان

This is probably the most famous month in the Islamic lunar calendar. During this month, Muslims are meant to focus on prayer, spirituality, charity, and fasting from sunrise to sunset. The last ten days of this month are called العَشرة الأواخِر.

Friday prayer	صَلاة الجُمعة

Muslims pray for about five minutes five times each day. These prayers are spread over fixed times of the day and so people in the Middle East will often use prayer times to set or describe arrangements . . .

Come to my house before sunset prayers.	تَعالَ إلى بَيتي قَبل صَلاة المَغرِب.
We went early; right after dawn prayers.	ذَهَبنا في الصّباح الباكِر بَعدَ صَلاة الفَجر مُباشَرَة.

EXERCISE

4·1

Ahmad gets confused, and often forgets what day it is. Help him by writing the correct day.

١ السَّمّاك مُغلَق يوم الأَحَد، وهو مُغلَق اليوم. غداً هو يوم _____

٢ أنا أزور أُمّي كل يوم جُمعة لِمُدّة ساعتَين. أنا زرتُ أُمّي أمس. اليوم هو يوم _____

٣ اليوم هو الأَربعاء، ونحن في المَساء. غداً هو يوم _____

٤ أنا أستَخدِم السيّارة يوم السبت. سَأستَخدِمها غداً. اليوم هو يوم _____

٥ كُلّ أُسبوع أَذهب إلى سوق الخُضار يوم الاثنين. أنا كُنتُ هُناك اليوم. أمس كان يوم _____

٦ يَبدَأ شَهر رَمَضان غداً. أوّل يوم هو الخميس. اليوم هو يوم _____

Complete the Arabic with a time phrase to match the English.

I go to the club once a week . . . ١

أَذهَب إلى النادي ــــــــــــــــــــــــــــــــــ

. . . but I never go on Sunday. ٢

ولكنّي لا أذهب ــــــــــــــــــــــــــ يوم الأحد.

Where's the manager? He left five minutes ago . . . ٣

أين المُدير؟ خَرَجَ ــــــــــــــــــــــــــــــــــ

. . . but he'll be back within an hour. ٤

ولكنّه سيَرجِع ــــــــــــــــــــــــــــــــــ

Most muslims perform the duty of the pilgrimage once in a lifetime. ٥

يُؤَدِّي أَغلَب المُسلِمين فَريضة الحَجّ ــــــــــــــــــــــــــــــــ

It seems that the journey will go on for ever. ٦

يبدو أن الرِّحلة سَتَستَمِرّ ــــــــــــــــــــــــــــــــ

I haven't seen a gas station for two hours. ٧

لَمْ أَرَ مَحَطّة بَنزين ــــــــــــــــــــــــــــــــــ

We will never arrive! ٨

لَنْ نَصِل ــــــــــــــــــــــــــ!

It's action time

to start	بَدَأَ/يَبدَأ
to finish (something else)	أَنهى/يُنهي
to (come to an) end	اِنتَهى/يَنتَهي
to postpone	أَجَّل/يُؤَجِّل
to continue	اِستَمَرّ/يَستَمِرّ
to suspend	عَلَّق/يُعَلِّق
to delay	أَخَّر/يُؤَخِّر
to wait	اِنتَظَر/يَنتَظِر
to set off	اِنطَلَق/يَنطَلِق
to hurry	أَسرَع/يُسرِع

When? مَتى؟

dawn	الفَجر
daybreak; first light	بُزوغ الفَجر
sunrise	الشُّروق
morning	الصَّباح
noon	الظُّهر
afternoon	بعد الظُّهر
sunset	الغُروب
twilight	شَفَق
evening	المَساء
midnight	مُنتَصَف اللَّيل
What time is it?	كَم الساعة؟
wristwatch	ساعة يَد
wall clock	ساعة حائِط
stopwatch	ساعة تَوقيت

EXERCISE
4·3

Match the 24-hour clocks with the times of day.

14:30	مُنتَصَف اللَّيل
12:00	الفَجر
00:00	الصَّباح
10:30	الظُّهر
05:30	بعد الظُّهر
19:00	الغُروب
19:30	الشَّفَق
21:30	المَساء

Nadia is describing a typical slice of her life. Select the suitable missing words and then fit them into the spaces provided.

أَطراف المَساء بيتي الظُّهر أَبدَأ الصباح أَنطَلِق المَطبَخ الفَجر

ـــــــ يومي في ـــــــ الباكِر. بَعد صَلاة ـــــــ مُباشرة، أَذهَب إلى ـــــــ

وأَتَناوَل الإفطار. ـــــــ في سيّارتي إلى المَطار في ـــــــ المدينة وأَعمَل هُناك حَتّى ـــــــ.

ثم أَتَّجِه إلى ـــــــ. يوم الجُمعة أُحِبّ أن أَلعَب التنس الساعة الثالثة بعد ـــــــ مع أُختي سميرة.

Handy extras

How old are you?	كَم عُمرك؟
Please! Don't waste your time there.	أَرجوكُم! لا تُضَيِّعوا وَقتَكم هُناك.
Did you cancel the trip due to time restrictions?	هل أَلْغَيْتُم الرِّحلة بِسَبَب ضيق الوقت؟
We'll try next time.	سَنُحاوِل في المَرّة القادِمة.

Local flavors

"God willing" is an important concept for Muslims in the Middle East. These expressions are usually part of their answer to many questions. Literally, they are . . .

if God wishes it to be so	إن شَاءَ الله
with God's permission	بِإذن الله
by God's command	بِأَمر الله

Firstly and lastly أَوَّلاً وأَخيراً

firstly	أَوَّلاً
lastly	أَخيراً
immediately	حالاً
during	أَثناء
gradually	بالتَّدريج
continuously	باستِمرار
in one go	في دُفعَة واحِدة
in the long term	على المَدى الطَّويل
in a fleeting moment	في لَحظَة عابِرَة

at any moment	في أَي لَحظة
at the end of the day	آخِر النَّهار
since yesterday	مُنذ أَمس
date	تاريخ/تَواريخ
era	عَهْد/عُهود
period	مُدّة/مُدَد
generation	جيل/أَجيال
timing	تَوقيت
stage	مَرحَلَة/مَراحِل
an additional stage	مَرحَلة إضافيّة
extra time	وَقت إضافيّ
suitable time	وَقت مُناسِب
first	أَوَّل/أَوائِل
last	آخِر/أَواخِر
consecutive	مُتَعاقِب
urgent	عاجِل
light-year	سَنة ضَوئيّة/سَنوات ضَوئيّة
in the dark	في الظَّلام
in broad daylight	في وَضَح النَهار

EXERCISE
4·5

Match the words and phrases to their opposites.

من وقت إلى آخَر	١ أوّلاً
على المدى الطويل	٢ الشروق
أوّل النهار	٣ في وضح النهار
الغروب	٤ بالتدريج
في الظلام	٥ وقت مناسب
في دفعة واحدة	٦ حالاً
أخيراً	٧ آخِر النهار
وقت غير مناسب	٨ باستمرار

Anwar is Nadia's neighbor. Read his side of the story.

مُنذُ حَوالي أَربعة شُهور، أو رُبَّما خمسة، كنتُ عند الشبّاك ورأيتُ هذه الفَتاة الجذّابة لأوّل مرّة. كان يوم جمعة،
وكانَت الساعة حوالي الثالثة بعد الظهر. فتاة مَلامِحها شرقيّة، وإبتِسامتها عريضة، وشعرها أَسود وناعِم وطويل.
كانَت تَلعَب التنس مع فتاة أُخرى. ذهبتُ إلى غرفة الجُلوس وبدأتُ أُخطِّط. أوّلًا، سَأَشتَري لها بعض الزهور.
زهور حَمراء. أو رُبَّما صَفراء أو زَرقاء. بعد ذلك سَأَطلُب منها أن تَتَناوَل الغداء معي يوم الأحد في مطعم سمك.
أو رُبَّما في مطعم إيطاليّ. ولكن، هل سَتُوافِق؟ رُبَّما.

EXERCISE 4·6

Now answer the questions.

1. When did Anwar see Nadia?

2. Where was he when he first saw her?

3. How does he describe Nadia's hair?

4. What was she doing when he saw her?

5. Where did Anwar plan his approach?

6. What is the first step in Anwar's plan?

7. What is the second step in Anwar's plan?

8. When is he planning to implement the second step?

It's action time

to cut	قَصّ/يَقُصّ
to wait	إِنتَظَر/يَنتَظِر
to expect	تَوَقَّع/يَتَوَقَّع
to persist	ثابَر/يُثابِر
to specify	حَدَّد/يُحَدِّد
to start	بَدَأ/يَبدَأ
to terminate	أَنهى/يُنهي
to shorten	قَصَّر/يُقَصِّر
to extend	أَطال/يُطيل
to abridge	إِختَصَر/يَختَصِر
to resist	قاوَم/يُقاوِم

Handy extras

last century	القَرن الماضي
next year	العام القادِم
this week	هذا الأُسبوع
until further notice	حَتّى إشعار آخَر
The age of wonder!	زَمَن العَجائِب!
They are arranged in chronological order.	إنّها مُرتَّبة حَسَبَ التَرتيب الزَّمني.
We are approaching the end of the season.	نَقتَرِب من نِهاية المَوسِم.
Everything here remains unchanged.	كُلّ شَيء هُنا لا يَزال بِلا تَغيير.
I was just about to go out.	كُنتُ على وَشَك الخُروج.

Local flavors

Here are two common Arabic expressions about time:

Time is like gold.	الوَقت من ذَهَب

This suggests time is precious because it is difficult to find.

Time is like the sword: if you don't cut it, it'll cut you.	الوَقت كَالسَّيف، إن لَم تَقطَعهُ، قَطَعك.

Is there a threat of violence here? I think I prefer the "gold" expression!

A lifetime طِوال العُمر

conception	تَخصيب
pregnancy	حَمل
fetus	جَنين/أَجِنّة
baby	رَضيع/رُضَّع
childhood	طُفولة
puberty	بُلوغ
adolescence	مُراهَقة
youthfulness	شَباب
adulthood	رُشد
manhood	رُجولة
maturity	نُضج
old-age	شَيخوخة
death	وَفاة

Handy extras

date of birth	تاريخ الميلاد
birth certificate	شَهادة الميلاد
death certificate	شَهادة وَفاة
from cradle to grave	مِن المَهد إلى اللَّحد
In the blink of an eye!	في لَمح البَصَر
new year's eve	لَيلة رَأس السَّنة
duration of the call	مُدّة المُكالَمة
on time	في المَوعِد
timetable	جدوَل المواعيد/جَداوِل المواعيد
I have an appointment with her.	عِندي مَوعِد مَعَها.
Sorry! I'm late!	آسِف! تَأَخَّرتُ!

EXERCISE 4·7

An ace secret agent has been observing Anwar as he prepares to meet Nadia for the first time. Check his notes and select the correct translation.

١ أمس كان عند الحلّاق لِيَحلَق شَعرهُ ولِحيَتهُ.

Yesterday, he went to the swimming pool early in the morning.

Yesterday, he was at the barber to cut his hair and beard.

Tomorrow he will be at the airport to greet his accountant.

٢ اليوم ذهب إلى مَحَلّ الزهور في الصباح الباكِر قبل أن يَتَناوَل الإفطار.

Today, he went to the flower shop early in the morning, before breakfast.

Tomorrow, he will be at the window watching the tennis game after breakfast.

Yesterday, at the restaurant he ordered everything on the menu for lunch.

٣ اشتَرى الكثير من الزهور الحمراء والصفراء والزرقاء.

He bought lots of purple, pink, and red flowers.

He borrowed his cousin's red sports car and blue hat.

He bought lots of red, yellow, and blue flowers.

٤ أنوَر يَجلِس الآن على الأريكة أمام ساعة الحائِط.

Anwar is about to eat lunch by the fireplace.

Anwar is now sitting on the sofa in front of the wall clock.

Anwar is now getting ready to play tennis.

Time **55**

٥ أنور على وَشك الخُروج في أيّ لَحظة. إنّه يَتَّجِه نحو الباب!

Tomorrow, he will repair the green door. He is at the window!

Anwar is about to go out any moment. He's going towards the door!

Yesterday he returned at midnight. He has bought so many flowers!

٦ أنور عاد إلى الأريكة. أَجَّلَ كلّ شيء إلى يوم الجمعة القادِم.

Friday is his day off. He has gone to sleep on the sofa.

Anwar has bought a new sofa. He will buy a new chair later on Friday.

Anwar has returned to the sofa. He postponed everything to next Friday.

Local flavors

The verb generally used for "to become" (أَصبَح/يُصبِح) originally means "to become by morning," and is formed from the same root as the word for "morning" (صَباح). There are less common equivalents linked to other times of the day:

to become (by evening, from مَساء meaning "evening")   أَمسى/يُمسي

to become (by mid-morning, from ضَحوة meaning "mid-morning/forenoon")   أَضحَى/يُضحي

EXERCISE
4·8

In each group, there are two people who have similar views or habits, and one who differs. See if you can spot the one who differs.

١

سَيَخرُج آدَم من البيت الآن ويَذهَب بِسُرعة إلى محطّة القطار.

سَأَخرُج فوراً من الباب وآخُذ السيّارة وأَنطَلِق إلى المطار!

سيَتَناوَل حَسَن الغَداء في الشُرفة، ثمّ يَجلِس على الأريكة لِمُدّة ساعتَين.

٢

يُحِبّ عُمَر عيد رأس السنة وأعياد الميلاد والمُناسَبات الاجتماعيّة.

أَرجوكُم! لا تُضَيِّعوا وَقتي. أنا لا أُحِبّ الجيران والأُسرة والأصدِقاء.

تَذهَب أمينة إلى كلّ الحَفلات الخَيريّة وحَفلات الزَّواج والخُطوبة.

٣

يذهب إبراهيم إلى الخَبّاز في الظلام، بعد غُروب الشمس.

تحبّ سميرة أن تَشتَري الزهور يومياً بعد صَلاة الفَجر.

كلّ يوم خميس، تذهب أمّي إلى السمّاك في الصباح الباكر.

٤

تَعالوا كلّكُم إلى بيتي بعد الصلاة وسَنَتَناوَل الغداء في حَديقتنا الفسيحة.

عندي مَأدُبة كبيرة في بيتي كلّ مَرّة شهر للأقارب والأولاد والأحفاد.

لا نُريد الضُيوف في بيتنا، ولكنّنا سنُعطي لكلّ ضَيف زَيتونة.

٥

سارة عندها سِباحة يوم السبت والثلاثاء، وجودو الجمعة والأربعاء وجولف الأحد.

بَدَأَت فريدة في لَعِب التنس والبولو والجولف مُنذُ خمس سنوات وسَتَستَمِرّ إن شاء الله.

تحبّ جيهان الجُلوس في غرفتها، ولكنّها تذهب إلى المطبخ أو الحمّام من وقت إلى آخر.

٦

يَعمَل كريم طَوال النهار في مَطبَعة وفي المساء يعمل في مطعم.

سَتَجِد هشام في المصنع باِستِمرار، من شُروق الشمس حتى مُنتَصَف الليل.

إسماعيل عنده بيت كبير في الضُواحي، سَتَجِده هناك عند حمّام السِّباحة.

EXERCISE 4·9

Join the following to create a logical sentence.

في اتّجاه الجسر.	١ هذه مناسبة نادرة جدّاً. إنّها
حاوِل يوم السبت.	٢ أَسرَعَ في سيّارته الجديدة
منذ خمس دقائق فقط.	٣ أرجوكم! لا تُضَيِّعوا وَقتَكم هنا
مَرّة في العُمر.	٤ النَّفَق مُغلِق يوم الجمعة
أنا لا أحبّ الحفلات.	٥ المَرحَلة الأولى كانت أمس، ولكن
المَرحَلة الإضافيّة غداً.	٦ تَأَخَّرتَ قليلاً. عاد إلى بيته

Complete the English to match the Arabic.

١ سَنَنْتَظِر هنا حَتَّى الغُروب.

We will _____ here until _____ .

٢ وَدَدْتُ أن أُصبِح مُهَندِساً طوال عُمري.

I've wanted to _____ an engineer all my _____ .

٣ سَأقول لكُم كلّ شيء في الوقت المُناسِب.

I'll tell you _____ at a suitable _____ .

٤ مَرحَلة المُراهَقة هي مَرحَلة صَعبة في حَياة الإنسان.

The stage of _____ is a _____ stage in the _____ of a person.

٥ سَأعود غداً ومعي شَهادة ميلادي.

I'll come back _____ with my _____ certificate.

٦ هل كُنتُم على وَشك الخُروج حالاً؟

Were you just _____ to go out _____ ?

As a man of wisdom, I have been advising Anwar as he struggles to meet Nadia for the first time. Check my notes and select the correct translation.

Anwar, next week is a very special week. ١

أنور، الأسبوع القادِم هو أسبوع خاصّ جدّاً.

أنور، العام القادِم سيكون هنا في أيّ لَحظة.

أنور، لا تجلس في الشرفة أو على الأريكة لمُدّة ساعة.

Go to the garden center early on Friday. ٢

اِذهَب إلى المصنع يوم الجمعة مع كريم وآدم.

اِذهَب إلى المَشتَل يوم الجمعة في الصباح الباكِر.

اِذهَب إلى المَشتَل يوم الأحد في وِضح النهار.

Buy lots of flowers. Red, yellow, and blue. ٣

اِشتَرِ الكثير من الزهور. أمي تحبّ الزهور.

سارة عندها سباحة يوم السبت. الجمعة والثلاثاء والأربعاء.

اِشتَرِ الكثير من الزهور. حمراء وصفراء وزرقاء.

Anwar, this is a rare, once-in-a-lifetime occasion. ٤

أنور، أُريدك أن تتناول الإفطار في المطبخ.

أنور، هذه مناسبة نادرة، مرّة في العمر.

أنور، هذه مناسبة عائلِيّة، مرّة في العمر.

Suspend everything and go to the entrance at three. ٥

تَعالى إلى بيتي قبل الساعة الثالثة.

عَلِّق كلّ شيء واِذهَب إلى المدخل في الثالثة.

أين جَدوَل المواعيد، نَقتَرِب من نهاية الموسِم.

Don't sit on the sofa, and try to be punctual! ٦

لا تجلس على الأريكة وحاوِل أن تأتي في الموعِد!

سنحاوِل في المَرّة القادِمَة، وحاوِل أن تجلس على الأريكة.

اِجلِس أنت على الأريكة. حاوِل أن تُحادِث جَدّتها.

Eating and drinking
الجُزء الخامِس: الأكل والشُّرب

Eating and drinking are activities that can unite people in a joyful celebration of life. However, people have also been known to fight over ownership of agricultural plots, water wells, fishing rights, pasture land, ownership of cattle, price of crops, and even restaurant bills.

Some food items have been so successful nearly all over the world that they have kept their names in most languages. Of these we could mention:

pizza	بيتزا
spaghetti	إِسباجيتّي
burger	بورجِر
ice cream	آيس كريم
falafel	فلافِل
omelet	أُومليت

Popular foods أَطعِمَة مَحبوبة

fish	سَمَك
chicken	دَجاج
rice	أَرُزّ
bread	خُبز
meat	لَحم
French fries	بَطاطِس مُحَمَّرة
vegetables	خُضرَوات
fruit	فَواكِه
cheese	جُبن
macaroni	مَكرونة

Local flavors

tahina (sesame seed dip)	طَحينة
Halal	حَلال

Halal meat is generally meat from animals that have been slaughtered according to Islamic law. In a broader sense, Halal can refer to anything that has been acquired in a legitimate way.

أَساسِيَّات Basics

onions	بَصَل
garlic	ثوم
celery	كَرَفس
carrots	جَزَر
tomatoes	طَماطِم
olive oil	زَيت زَيتون
salt	مِلح
pepper	فِلفِل
stock	مَرَق
coriander	كُزبَرَة
parsley	بَقدونِس
thyme	زَعتَر
flour	دَقيق
eggs	بَيض
butter	زُبد
lemons	لَيمون

Handy extras

Many Arabic words for vegetables, fruits, and animals are group, or "collective," words. They refer to a group of "fish," "carrots," "eggs," etc., or to these items in general.

If you want to talk about a *single* fish, carrot or egg, add the ending ة (-*a*) to the group word:

a fish	سَمَكة
the carrot	الجَزَرة
this egg	هذه البَيضة

Local flavors

"Green" is sometimes used to mean "fresh," as opposed to "dried":

fresh coriander	كُزبَرَة خَضراء

Help me remember what I bought from these outlets by circling the right food item and write it down in the space provided.

the fishmonger ــــــــــــــ ١

بَصَل/بَيض/سَمَك

the grocery store ــــــــــــــ ٢

خُضرَوات/زُبد/جُزر

the bakery ــــــــــــــ ٣

لَيمون/أوملِيت/خُبز

the green grocer ــــــــــــــ ٤

طَماطِم/دَقيق/بورجِر

the restaurant ــــــــــــــ ٥

دَجاج وبَطاطِس مُحَمَّرة/كُزبَرة خَضراء/مِلح

the butcher ــــــــــــــ ٦

آيس كريم/زَيت زَيتون/لَحم

the pizzeria ــــــــــــــ ٧

زَعتَر/ثوم/بيتزا

Preparation الإعداد

raw	نَيِّء
cooked	مَطبوخ
fresh	طازَج
frozen	مُجَمَّد
canned	مُعَلَّب
smoked	مُدَخَّن
dried	مُجَفَّف
marinated	مُتَبَّل
grilled	مشويّ

fried	مَقْلِيّ
boiled	مَسلوق
chopped	مُقَطَّع
soaked	مَنقوع
minced	مَفروم
peeled	مُقَشَّر
stuffed	مَحشو
in tomato sauce	بِصَلصة الطَّماطِم
cubes	مُكَعَّبات
slices	شَرائِح
organic	عُضوِيّ
ready to eat	جاهِز للأكل

Local flavors

skewer	سيخ/أسياخ
over charcoal	على الفَحم
baked (in the oven)	في الفُرن
baked in a clay pot	طاجِن

EXERCISE
5·2

What's on the menu today? Match the Arabic with the English.

raw fish with Japanese rice	١ مكونة مع اللحم
omelet with fresh parsley	٢ جُبن أبيض مع الزيتون الأسود
fresh vegetables from the market	٣ الدجاج المشوي على الفحم
macaroni with minced meat	٤ الخضروات الطازجة من السوق
white cheese with black olives	٥ سمك نيّء مع الأرزّ اليابانيّ
chicken grilled over charcoal	٦ أومليت مع البقدونس الأخضر

Work out what these combinations are.

١ مكرونة باللحم المفروم وصلصة الطماطم

_____

٢ بيض عضويّ بالثوم والزعتر

_____

٣ شرائح السمك المشوي مع الكرفس والكزبرة الخضراء

_____

٤ دجاج متبّل محشو بالجزر والبقدونس

_____

٥ لحم مفروم مع الجبن والبقدونس المجفّف

_____

٦ فلافل البيت مع أومليت البصل المدخّن

_____

It's action time

to wash	غَسَل/يَغسِل
to cook	طَبَخ/يَطبُخ
to peel	قَشَّر/يُقَشِّر
to chop	خَرَّط/يُخَرِّط
to dice	قَطَّع/يُقَطِّع
to boil	غَلى/يَغلي
to grill	شَوى/يَشوي
to fry	قَلى/يَقلي
to roast	حَمَّص/يُحَمِّص
to marinade	تَبَّل/يُتَبَّل
to mince	فَرَم/يَفرُم
to stuff	حَشى/يَحشو
to grate	بَشَر/يَبشُر

to add	أَضاف/يُضيف
to stir	قَلَّب/يُقَلِّب
to thicken	كثَّف/يُكَثِّف
to dilute	خَفَّف/يُخَفِّف

Here are groups of three words. Circle the odd one out in each group.

١ يشوي/يقلي/بيضة

٢ بقدونس/متبّل/مدخّن

٣ كزبرة/سمك/زعتر

٤ زيت زيتون/مكعّبات/مرق

٥ ملح/أومليت/بيض مقليّ

٦ جزر/أرزّ/مكرونة

Bruno, the stressed-out chef, is barking out instructions at hapless Mo, the new kitchen boy. Help Mo by selecting the right Arabic.

Dice the carrots then peel the potatoes! ١

أُسلُق الدجاج بعد أن تُقَطِّع الجزر!

قَطِّع هذه الجزرة قبل أن تُقَطِّع البطاطس!

قَطِّع الجزر ثمّ قَشِّر البطاطس!

Stir the stock while you thicken the tomato sauce! ٢

كثِّف الطماطم وقَلِّب الدجاج وقَشِّر البطاطس!

قَلِّب المرق وأنت تُكَثِّف صلصة الطماطم!

قَلِّب المرق وأنت تُقَطِّع البطاطس والكرفس!

Don't add the garlic before you dilute the tomatoes first! ٣

لا تُضيف الثوم قبل أن تُقَطِّع البطاطس أوّلاً!

لا تُقَطِّع البطاطس قبل أن تُضيف الجزر أوّلاً!

لا تُضيف الثوم قبل أن تُخَفِّف الطماطم أوّلاً!

Grate the cheese before you stuff the chicken! ٤

أُبشُر الجبن بعد أن تَبشُر الجزر!

أُبشُر الجبن قبل أن تَحشو الدجاج!

قَطِّع الدجاج قبل أن تَبشُر البطاطس!

Give me the chicken slices, and quickly mince this meat! ٥

أعطِني هذه الخضروات بسرعة ثمّ خَفِّف الطماطم!

أعطِني شرائح الدجاج وأُفرُم هذا اللحم بسرعة!

خُذ شرائح الطماطم بسرعة بعد أن تُقَطِّع الدجاج!

Wash then roast these vegetables while you are grilling this fish! ٦

اِغسَل ثمّ حَمِّص هذه الخضروات وأنت تَشوي هذه الدجاجة!

اِشوِ هذه الدجاجة قبل أن تَغسِل الجزر وتُضيف البصل!

اِغسَل ثمّ حَمِّص هذه الخضروات وأنت تَشوي هذه السمكة!

The chef has recommended this week's menu to the restaurant manager. Read his notes.

الاثنين: مكرونة مع دجاج في الفرن

الثلاثاء: بورجر مع الجزر المسلوق والبطاطس المحمّرة

الأربعاء: بيض أومليت بالبقدونس وباللحم المفروم وبالبصل المحمّر مع الخضروات المسلوقة

الخميس: سباجيتي بصلصة الطماطم مع الجبن والكزبرة الخضراء الطازجة

الجمعة: شرائح لحم بالثوم وبالزعتر وبزيت الزيتون مع أرزّ

السبت: سمك مشويّ، متبّل بالزيت والليمون وشرائح البرتقال الطازج

الأحد: المطبخ مغلق، ولكن المطعم يقدّم ...

البيتزا

خبز محمّص مع زبد

شاي أخضر أو أحمر

برتقال

ليمون

كولا

Now answer these questions.

1. How is the chicken cooked on Monday?

2. Are the carrots and potatoes cooked the same way on Tuesday?

3. What three ingredients are added to the omelette on Wednesday?

4. What does the chef suggest for Thursday?

5. How is the meat flavored on Friday?

6. What goes into the marinade on Saturday?

7. What happens at the restaurant on Sundays?

Based on the menu above, fill out the logical day of the week in the space provided.

١ أنا أحبّ السمك المشوي. سأذهب يوم _____

٢ أنا أحبّ الاسباجيتي. سأذهب يوم _____

٣ أنا أحبّ البورجر. سأذهب يوم _____

٤ أنا لا أحبّ البيض. لن أذهب يوم _____

٥ أنا أحبّ الأرزّ. سأذهب يوم _____

٦ أنا أحبّ البيتزا. سأذهب يوم _____

٧ أنا أحبّ الدجاج. سأذهب يوم _____

Around the kitchen حّول المّطبّخ

meal	وَجبَة/وَجَبات
utensils	أداة/أدوات
pot	حَلّة/حِلَل
basket	سَلّة/سِلال
steam	بُخار
hot	ساخِن
cold	بارِد
spices	بُهارات

herbs	تَوابِل
handful	حِفنة
dough	عَجين

It's action time

to shop	تَسَوَّق/يَتَسَوَّق
to soak	نَقَع/يَنقَع
to mix	خَلَط/يَخلِط
to serve	قَدَّم/يُقَدِّم
to freeze	جَمَّد/يُجَمِّد
to kneed	عَجَن/يَعجِن
to bake	خَبَز/يَخبِز

EXERCISE 5·8

Here are the chef's notes for a chicken and vegetable soup recipe. Unfortunately, they are muddled. Can you put them in the right order?

حَساء الخُضرَوات والدَّجاج

chicken and vegetable soup

غَلَيتُ بعض الماء والملح وبصلة في حَلّة كبيرة.

بعد ذلك، كان الحَساء جاهِزاً للأكل.

عُدتُ إلى البيت وذَهَبتُ إلى المطبخ.

غَسَلتُ وقَطَّعتُ الخضروات ثمّ أَضَفتُها للدجاجة.

ذَهَبتُ إلى السوق في الصباح الباكر.

تَرَكتُ الحَلّة على نار هادِئة لمِدّة ساعة ونِصف.

اِشتَرَيتُ خضروات المَوسِم ودجاجة كبيرة.

قَطَّعتُ الدجاجة ووَضَعتُها في الماء المَغلي.

Local flavors

One of the most popular dishes in Yemen and Saudi Arabia is lamb, wrapped in foil, then buried under the sand with burning ambers in an airtight pot. The same method is also used to cook beans in Upper Egypt.

Different people and regions enjoy eating different foods. Person "A" may enjoy eating something that fills person "B" with dread and horror. A valued, high-table delicacy in region "X" can be a cute, cuddly, cherished little pet in region "Y," or a reviled pest in region "Z."

Rabbit (أَرْنَب/أَرانِب), pigeon (حَمامة/حَمام), goat (عَنزة/عَنز ;ماعِز/مَواعِز), and camel (جَمَل/جِمال) are often eaten in the Middle East, although not necessarily so elsewhere.

Donkey (حِمار/حَمير), horse (حِصان/أَحصِنة) and frog (ضَفدَع/ضَفادِع) are eaten in Europe but not knowingly eaten in the Middle East.

Jews and Muslims do not eat pork (لَحم الخِنزير), and have strict rules about the slaughtering of all animals.

Around another kitchen حَولَ مَطبَخ آخَر

beetroot	بَنجَر
peas	بازِلّاء
eggplant	باذِنجان
artichokes	خَرشوف
cardamom	حَبّ الهال
basil	ريحان
ginger	زَنجَبيل
turmeric	كُركُم
saffron	زَعْفَران
cumin	كَمّون
pine nut	صَنوبَر
root	جِذر/جُذور
grain	حَبّة/حَبّات
almond	لَوزة/لوز
hazelnut	بُندُقة/بُندُق
walnut (literally "camel's eye")	عَين جَمَل

Handy extras

To be soaked in cold water until morning.	يُنقَع في الماء البارِد حتّى الصباح.
Let it stand for an hour before cutting it into slices.	دَعوه يَهدَأ لمُدّة ساعة قَبل تَقطيعه إلى شَرائِح.
Mix all the ingredients in a large bowl.	اِخلِطوا كلّ المُكوّنات في وِعاء كَبير.

Leave it to cool down completely.	أُتركُوه لِيَبرَد تَماماً.
Serve immediately.	قَدِّموه فَوراً.
Put them to one side.	أُتركُوها جانِباً.
About a teaspoon.	مِقدار مِلعَقة شاي.

Mo has been taking notes for various recipes and cooking techniques. Unfortunately, they are muddled. Can you help by choosing the right Arabic?

fresh, frozen, smoked, or dried ١

طازِج، مسلوق، مُحَمَّر أو مُجَفَّف

مُجَفَّف، مُدَخَّن، طازَج، أو مُجَمَّد

طازَج، مُجَمَّد، مُدَخَّن أو مُجَفَّف

ready to eat immediately ٢

اِخلِطوا كلّ المُكَوِّنات

جاهِز للأكل فَوراً

وضعتُها في الماء

leave it to boil for five minutes ٣

أُتركُوه ليغلي لِمّدة خمس دقائق

جاهِز للأكل بعد خمس دقائق

أُتركُوها جانباً لِمّدة خمس دقائق

serve with rice or macaroni ٤

اِخلِطوا الأرز مع المكرونة

أضيفوا الأرز أو المكرونة

قَدِّموه مع الأرزّ أو المكرونة

add the fried onion, garlic, and chicken stock ٥

اِخلِطوا كلّ المُكَوِّنات مع البصل ومَرَق الدجاج

أضيفوا البصل المحمّر، والثوم ومَرَق الدجاج

جَهِّزوا الماء المغلي مع البصل ثمّ أُتركُوه لِيَبرَد

chop the fresh parsley, celery, and coriander ٦

قَطِّعوا البقدونس الأخضر والكرفس والكزبرة

اخلِطوا الثوم مع البصل و اُتركوه ليغلي

قَطِّعوا البقدونس المُجَفَّف مع الكرفس

soak the almonds and hazelnuts in a large bowl ٧

اِخلِطوا العجين مع الزبد في سلّة كبيرة

اِنقَعوا البندق مع التوابل في زجاجة كبيرة

اِنقَعوا اللوز مع البندق في وَعاء كبير

Some fruit? بَعض الفاكِهة؟

grapes	عِنَب
bananas	مَوز
oranges	بُرتُقال
berries	توت
plums	بَرقوق
watermelons	بَطّيخ
melons	شَمّام
dates	تَمر
apples	تُفّاح
figs	تين
pomegranates	رُمّان

Handy extras

Remember, to talk about a single fruit add the ending ة (-a) to the group word:

an apple	تُفّاحة
a banana	المَوزة

Drinks المشروبات

tea	شاي
coffee	قَهوة
fruit juice	عَصير فَواكِه
water	ماء
lemonade	لَيمونادة

cola	كولا
milk	حَليب
hot chocolate	شوكولاتة ساخِنة
cocoa	كاكاو
chamomile	بابونج
beer	بيرة
wine	نَبيذ
spirits	مَشروبات رَوحيّة
slice of lemon	شَريحة لَيمون/شَرائِح لَيمون
slice of orange	شَريحة بُرتُقال/شَرائِح بُرتُقال

Handy extras

without ice	بِدون ثَلج
bottle of cola	رُجاجة كولا
glass of water	كوب ماء
cup of tea	فِنجان شاي
strong tea (literally, heavy tea)	شاي ثَقيل
weak tea (literally, light tea)	شاي خَفيف
tea with milk	شاي بالحَليب
mint tea	شاي بالنَّعناع
iced tea	شاي بالثَّلج
Turkish coffee, no sugar	قَهوة سادة
Turkish coffee, little sugar	قَهوة على الريحة
Turkish coffee, medium sugar	قَهوة مَظبوط
Turkish coffee, extra sugar	قَهوة سُكَّر زيادة
whole milk	حَليب كامِل الدَّسَم
skim milk	حَليب مَنزوع الدَّسَم

Note that cappuccino, expresso, latte, etc., are known by their European names:

كابوتشينو، اكسبرسو، لاتي

Local flavors

sugar cane juice	عَصير قَصَب السُّكَّر
guava juice	عَصير جوافة
lemon juice	عَصير لَيمون

Match these drinks with their opposites.

كوب نبيذ أبيض	قهوة بالحليب
قهوة سكّر زيادة	كوب ماء بارد
قهوة بدون حليب	شاي خفيف
كولا بدون ثلج	زجاجة بيرة صغيرة
كوب ماء ساخن	كولا بالثلج
شاي ثقيل	قهوة سادة
زجاجة بيرة كبيرة	كوب نبيذ أحمر

You are a beleaguered bartender. Work out what each table wants and complete the order.

١ المائدة رقم واحد: ثلاث زجاجات كولا، كوب من عصير البرتقال الطازج، وزجاجة ماء.

Table one:

3 x _____

1 x _____

1 x _____

٢ المائدة رقم اثنين: ستّ زجاجات ليمونادة، كوب من عصير قصب السكّر، وفنجان شاي بالثلج.

Table two:

6 x _____

1 x _____

1 x _____

٣ المائدة رقم ثلاثة: زجاجة بيرة، ثلاث أطباق بطاطس محمّرة، شوكولاتة ساخنة، أربعة أكواب من عصير الليمون بشرائح الليمون.

Table three:

1 x _____

3 x _____

1 x _____

4 x _____

Eating and drinking   **73**

٤ المائدة رقم أربعة: فنجان شاي بالحليب، فنجان قهوة تركي سكّر زيادة، شاي بالنعناع، وكوب من النبيذ الأبيض.

Table four:

1 x _____

1 x _____

1 x _____

1 x _____

٥ المائدة رقم خمسة: كوب ماء مع شريحة برتقال، كوب فارغ، وفنجان شاي أخضر بدون سكّر.

Table five:

1 x _____

1 x _____

1 x _____

٦ المائدة رقم ستة: الأسبوعيّ الخاصّ لثلاثة، وكوب من عصير الطماطم بالملح والفلفل.

Table six:

3 x _____

1 x _____

EXERCISE 5·12

Jihan's mother is preparing for her daughter's birthday party. Fill in the missing words.

الجبن   المبشور   بصلصة   ثلاث   الفحم   عصير   بالثلج   دجاجات

١ تَسَوَّقتُ صباح اليوم واشتريتُ ستّ _____ من السوق.

٢ سأشوي ثلاث دجاجات على _____، وسأطبخ _____ دجاجات في الفرن.

٣ سأُقَدِّم الدجاج مع بعض المكرونة _____ الطماطم و _____.

٤ سأُقَدِّم لضيوف جيهان الكولا _____ و _____ البرتقال والآيس كريم.

Mimi is a fly on the wall in a restaurant. Read this extract from her diary.

اليوم، جاءَ رَجُل بَدين، رَقَبَتهُ قصيرة ويَطنهُ كُرَوِيّ، وله شارب كثيف، وجَلَسَ على المائدة رقم ثمانية بِجوار الشبّاك. إنّه جَشِع! طَلَبَ المَرَق والسمك المَقلي والدجاج واللحم المشوي على الفحم. ثمّ طَلَبَ بطاطس محمّرة في الفرن وبطاطس مسلوقة بالزيت والليمون والزَّعتَر، مع طَبَق من الأرزّ ويبعض المكرونة بصَلصة الطماطم واللحم المفروم، وطَبَق آخر من المكرونة ولكن غَطّاهُ بالزُّبد والريحان. أنا أرى من هنا أن هناك بعض قِطَع الدجاج الطَريّ على شارِبه. اليوم، أنا سَأَتَناوَل الغداء على شاربه الكثيف لأنّني أحبّ الدجاج الطَريّ!

Decide which of the sentences about Mimi's diary is true and which is false.

1. The greedy customer had a long neck. (T/F)

2. He sat at table number seven by the door. (T/F)

3. He ordered a lot of dishes, including fried fish. (T/F)

4. He ordered two different plates of macaroni. (T/F)

5. The greedy customer appears to like potatoes a lot. (T/F)

6. There were bits of basil stuck to his beard. (T/F)

7. Mimi is planning to have chicken for lunch today. (T/F)

Education

الجُزء السادِس: التَّعليم

It might be a good idea to start this unit with highlighting the root ج/م/ع (j-m-ع) which, broadly, is to do with collecting, combining, or gathering. It is a wonderful example of the root system and how efficient it can be in building up vocabulary. Let's start with the verb:

to collect	جَمَع/يَجمَع

Now here are some examples of the flexibility of this verb:

The maths teacher is **adding up** the numbers.	مُدَرِّس الرِّياضيّات يَجمَع الأرقام
The nurse is **collecting** the donations.	المُمَرِّضة تَـجمَع التَبَرُّعات
The director is **gathering up** the actors.	المُخرِج يَجمَع المُمَثِّلين
My car **combines** speed and comfort.	سَيّارتي تَـجمَع بين السُرعة والرّاحة

There are many Arabic words and expressions that come from this root, again, all related in meaning:

the plural (in grammar)	الجَمْع
the total	المَجموع
the area's main mosque	الجامِع/الجَوامِع
Friday, the day on which Muslims gather for the main weekly prayer	الجُمعة
university	جامِعة/جامِعات
group	مَجموعة/مَجموعات
assembly	جَمعِيّة/جَمعِيّات
everybody	الجَميع
consensus	إجماع

76

meeting	اِجتِماع/اِجتِماعات
society/community	مُجتَمَع/مُجتَمَعات
sociology	عِلم الاِجتِماع
social status	الحالة الاِجتِماعيّة
the solar system	المَجموعة الشَّمسيّة
social animal	حَيَوان اِجتِماعيّ/حَيَوانات اِجتَماعيّة
benefits the community	يُفيد المُجتَمَع/يُفيد المُجتَمَعات

Around the school حَولَ المَدرَسة

school	مَدرسة/مَدارِس
primary	اِبتِدائيّ
secondary	ثانويّ
day nursery	دار حَضانة/دور حَضانة
kindergarten	رَوضة الأطفال/رِياض الأطفال
institute	مَعهَد/مَعاهِد
teacher	مُدرِّس/مُدرِّسون
instructor; teacher	مُعَلِّم/مُعَلِّمون
lecturer	مُحاضِر/مُحاضِرون
dean	عَميد/عُمَداء
inspector	مُفَتِّش/مُفَتِّشون
classroom	فَصل/فُصول
lesson	دَرس/دُروس
class (period)	حِصّة/حِصَص
syllabus	مَنهَج/مَناهِج
degree	شَهادة/شَهادات
studying	مُذاكَرة
revising	مُراجَعة
examination	اِمتِحان/اِمتِحانات
full marks	دَرَجات نِهائيّة

Nader is planning to write his life story, even though he is only twenty-one. His notes, however, have been shuffled. Can you help him put them back in the right chronological order?

ولأنّها أَبعَد، كُنتُ أَذهَب مع أبي في الصباح بالسيّارة

تَعَلَّمتُ كيف آخُذ المُواصَلات العامّة إلى مدرستي يوميّاً

أُريد أن أَستَمِرّ في دراسة الكومبيوتر وآخُذ الدكتوراة

أنا اِسمي نادر وعُمري الآن واحد وعشرون سَنة

وبعد ذلك سَيكون اِسمي دُكتور نادر. إنّه زَمَن العَجائِب!

وبعد ذلك ذَهَبتُ إلى مدرسة اِبتدائيّة في حَيّ أَبعَد قَليلاً

ولأنّها قَريبة، كُنتُ أَمشي إلى هُناك مع أمّي في الصباح

في البِداية، ذَهَبتُ إلى رَوضة أطفال قَريبة جدّاً من البيت

وبعد المَدارس دَخَلتُ الجامِعة وأَخَذتُ شهادة في الكومبيوتر

ولكن حين ذَهَبتُ إلى مدرسة ثانويّة في حَيّ بعيد جدّاً عن بيتنا

Join the following to create a logical sentence.

أُترُكي الجيتار جانباً.	١ يَجمَع المُمَرِّض التَبَرُّعات
والآن مُحاضِر في الجامعة.	٢ سَتَكون دار الحضانة الجديدة
أنني سَآخُذ الدَّرجات النِّهائيّة	٣ المُفَتِّشون يُريدون الاِجتِماع مع
للمُستَشفى الجديد.	٤ أنا أَخَذتُ شهادة الدكتوراة
أنّني سَآخُذ الدَّرجات النِّهائيّة.	٥ يا نادية! هذا وقت المُذاكَرة والمُراجَعة،
مُفيدة جدّاً للمُجتَمَع.	٦ هناك إجماع بين كلّ المُدَرِّسين

Which of the English sentences best represents the Arabic?

١ تَجمَع هذه المُمَرِّضة بين العَطف والسُرعة.

This car is fast but stable around bends.

This nurse collects fast cars.

This nurse combines kindness with speed.

٢ هذه المَجموعة جاءت من مدرسة واحدة وفَصل واحد.

This group came from different schools in different areas.

This group came from one school and one class.

This group came from the same class but from different schools.

٣ مَدينَتُهُم فيها مَعهَد واحد صغير لِتَدريس عِلم الاِجتِماع.

Their school has one small meeting room for teacher training.

Their town has one small institute for teaching sociology.

Their school has one small meeting room for teachers.

٤ يَجمع منير السيّارات القديمة وعِنده مَجموعة كبيرة مِنها.

Mounir collects old cars and has a large collection of them.

Mounir adds up all the costs then pays out in large checks.

Mounir is in the meeting room with the old car dealer.

٥ هذا المُخرج دَرَس السينما مَعنا في جامِعة بِرلين.

This exit door will take you to the Berlin Cinema.

This cinema near Berlin airport is a good place to meet.

This director studied cinema with us at Berlin University.

٦ أُريد أن أَدرُس العُلوم اَلّتي تُفيد المُجتَمَع.

I want to study history of science and sociology.

I want to study the sciences that benefit society.

I want to study with you but I must go to a meeting.

It's action time

to teach	عَلَّم/يُعَلِّم
to learn	تَعَلَّم/يَتَعَلَّم
to ask	سَأَل/يَسأَل
to reply	أَجاب/يُجيب
to think	فَكَّر/يُفَكِّر
to solve	حَلَّ/يَحُلَّ
to participate	شارَك/يُشارِك
to contribute	ساهَم/يُساهِم
to understand	فَهِم/يَفهَم
to concentrate	رَكَّز/يُرَكِّز
to explain	شَرَح/يَشرَح
to clarify	وَضَّح/يُوَضِّح
to absorb	اِستَوعَب/يَستَوعِب
to summarize	لَخَّص/يُلَخِّص
to know	عَرَف/يَعرِف
to lecture	حاضَر/يُحاضِر
to pass	نَجَح/يَنجَح
to fail	رَسَب/يَرسُب

Handy extras

optional subjects	مَوادّ اِختِياريّة
compulsory attendance	حُضور إجباريّ
private tuition	دُروس خُصوصيّة
reference books	مَراجِع
scholarship	مِنْحَة دِراسيّة
graduation ceremony	حَفل التَّخَرُّج
humanities	العُلوم الإنسانيّة

The history test is easy but long.	اِمتِحان التاريخ سَهل ولكنّه طويل.
We stayed up revising all night.	سَهِرنا نُراجِع طَوال الليل.
The Arabic teacher is lenient most of the time.	مُدَرِّس اللُّغة العَرَبيّة مُتَساهِل مُعظم الوقت.
My grades are slipping from bad to worse.	تَنزَلِق دَرَجاتي من سَيِّء إلى أَسوأً.

EXERCISE
6·4

In each of these groups of three sentences there are two describing similar situations and one that's clearly different. Try to identify the odd one out.

١ تُدَرِّس الدكتورة جيهان لنا عِلم الاجتِماع يوم الثلاثاء.

تُدَرِّس الدكتورة نيفين لنا التاريخ أيّام الإثنين والأربعاء والخميس.

تُدَرِّس الدكتورة مريم لنا اللغة العربيّة ثلاثة أيّام في الأسبوع.

٢ في الفصل، تَفهَم نادية شَرح المُدَرِّس.

في الفصل، يُرَكِّز أحمد دائماً في دُروسه.

في الفصل، يُفَكِّر نادر دائماً في نادية.

٣ يُذاكِر أصدِقائي طوال الليل.

يُذاكِر أولاد عَمّتي بعد الإفطار.

يُذاكِر جيراني حَتَّى صَلاة الفَجر.

٤ اِختارَت سميرة أن تَدرُس التاريخ لأنَّها تُحِبّه.

الرياضيّات يا إسماعيل من أهَمّ الموادّ الإجباريّة.

اِختَرتُ اللغة الفرنسيّة لأنَّها مادّة اِختياريّة.

٥ سَأَلَت المدرّسة دينا فَأَجابَتها بسُرعة.

تحبّ نيفين أن تُشارك وتَسأَل لتَتَعَلَّم.

منير لا يَسأَل ولا يُناقِش ولا يُفَكِّر.

٦ تَنزَلِق دَرَجات هشام من سَيِّء إلى أَسوَأ.

الإجماع هو أن بشير سَيَأخُذ الدَّرجات النِّهائيّة.

رَسَبَ فرانكو في اللغة العربيّة والرياضيّات والتاريخ.

Local flavors

Arabic grammar	النَّحو

The study of Arabic grammar and syntax is known as النَّحو. Amongst the specific aspects of this study are:

inflection (changes to words caused by the grammar of a sentence)	الصَّرف
grammatical case endings	الإعراب
vowelling	التَّشكيل
nunation, for example كِتابٌ (kitaab<u>un</u>)	التَّنوين
to elucidate	فَسَّر/يُفَسِّر
elucidating	تَفسير

التَّفسير (Tafsir) is one of the philosophical disciplines of Islam. It deals with the possible meaning, an individual's interpretation, the probable purpose, perceived significance, and likely implication of a verse in the Quran.

Inside the classroom داخِل الفَصل

pencil	قَلَم رَصاص/أقلام رَصاص
ruler	مِسطَرة/مَساطِر
board	سَبّورة/سَبّورات
dictionary	قاموس/قَواميس
rule; basis	قاعِدة/قَواعِد
the grammar of a language	قَواعِد اللُّغة
fact	حَقيقة/حَقائِق
synonym	مُرادِف/مُرادِفات
fable	خُرافة/خُرافات
legend	أُسطورة/أَساطير
achievement	إنجاز/إنجازات
mistake	خَطَأ/أَخطاء
result	نَتيجة/نَتائِج
style	أُسلوب/أَساليب
ambitious	طَموح/طَموحون
volunteer	مُتَطَوِّع/مُتَطَوِّعون

Choose the appropriate ending.

١ أحمد طَموح لأنّه ...

يحبّ أن يُثَرثِر مع الحلّاق.

يريد شهادة الدكتوراة في عُلوم الكمبيوتر.

يحبّ المكرونة والبخور والأفلام القديمة.

٢ جاكسون عنده قاموس في سيّارته لأنّه ...

يدرُس اللغة العربيّة في مَعهَد بعيد عن بيته.

يأكُل الدجاج المشويّ على الفحم كلّ يوم أحد.

يريد أن يأخُذ الدَرَجات النهائيّة في الرياضيّات.

٣ كلّ أصدقائي يُذاكِرون ويُراجِعون لأنّ ...

الامتحانات كانَت في الشهر الماضي.

الامتحانات سَتَبدَأ في الأسبوع القادم.

هناك حَفل خيريّ كبير في الحديقة العامّة.

٤ الذهاب إلى المَلجَأ ليس إجباريّاً لأنَّ ...

الفُصول كلّها مُغلَقة في الشِّتاء.

العُمّال هناك كلّهم مُتَطَوِّعون.

جَدوَل المَواعيد عِند مَدخَل الجامعة.

٥ أنا لا أَفهَم ما تقوله كلوديت لأنّني ...

لا أُحبّ أن أَبدأ قَبل الساعة الثامنة.

أُحبّ أن أَقرأ كُتُب الأساطير والخُرافات.

لم أَدرُس اللّغة الفَرنسيّة في المدرسة.

٦ لَن تَذهَب كريمة إلى حَفل التَّخَرُّج لأنّها ...

فتاة جذّابة ومَلامِحها شرقيّة.

عندها قلم رصاص أزرق جديد.

رَسَبَت في خمسة موادّ من ستّة.

Mario is a busy Italian student of Arabic. Read this entry from his diary.

يَبدَأ نَهاري في السادسة والنصف. أَشرَب فِنجان قَهوة بالحليب ثمّ آخُذ سيّارتي القديمة إلى مَعهَد دراسات اللغة العربيّة الموجود بجوار الفَنارة الكبيرة عند الميناء. أنا طالب هناك، وأَدرُس اللغة العربيّة في فترة الصباح. القاموس وكُتُب المراجع دائماً بجانبي، ولكن أحيانا أَسأَل العميد، الدكتور موسى، أو أَسأَل مدرّستي الدكتورة زينب. أنا أَحِبّ الدكتورة زينب جدّاً لأنّها مُتَساهِلة وتحبّ الابتِسام وهي تَشرَح في الفصل.

بعد المعهد أَتَناوَل الغداء في مطعم إيطاليّ. أنا أَحِبّ المكرونة بصلصة الطماطم مثل جميع الإيطاليّين. وبعد الظهر أَحِبّ أن أُراجِع أَخطائي في الكلمات العربيّة وأُسلوبي في الكتابة، وأدرس الجَمع. في المساء أَعود إلى شقّتي وأَجلِس على الأَريكة وأُشاهِد الأفلام المصريّة القديمة بالأبيض والأسود وآكُل إِسباجيتي أو أي شيء بسيط في الثّلاجة.

EXERCISE 6·6

Now decide what is true and what is false.

1. Mario has a shiny new Italian sports car. (T/F)

2. The institute where he studies Arabic is near the port. (T/F)

3. The dean is called Dr. Zeinab. (T/F)

4. Mario revises the plurals before lunch. (T/F)

5. Dr. Moussa teaches Italian to Chinese students. (T/F)

6. At night, Mario raids the fridge for something simple to eat. (T/F)

EXERCISE 6·7

The following sentences are loosely based on the above diary. Select the Arabic that best represents the English.

١ My day starts at seven.

يبدأ نَهاري في السابعة.

أَدرُس سبَعة أيام في الأَسبوع.

أُذاكِر سَبع ساعات كلّ يوم.

٢ The teacher likes my writing style.

تُحِبّ المُدَرِّسة أُسلوبي في الكتابة.

سأَكتُب لُمُدّة ساعة ثمّ أَقرَأ هذا الكتاب.

أنا أُحِبّ أُسلوب المُدَرِّسة في الكتابة.

I am a student at the institute of French language. ٣

أنا وزميلي نُراجِع دُروس اللغة الفرنسيّة كلّ يوم.

أنا طالب في معهد دراسات اللغة الفرنسيّة.

أنا طالب في مَعهد دراسة التاريخ الفرنسيّ.

In the afternoon I revise the plurals. ٤

أنا أُراجِع الجَمع بعد الغداء.

أنا أُراجِع الجَمع بعد الظُّهر.

سأجمَع دُروسي وأُراجِعها مَعكُم.

The dictionary is always in my car. ٥

سأبحَث عن هذه الكَلِمة في القاموس.

القاموس دائماً في سيّارتي.

السيّارة عند الباب بجوار المدخل.

Sometimes I ask the dean. ٦

أحياناً أرى العميد في المعهد.

عِندي سُؤال للعميد والمُدَرِّسة.

أحياناً أَسأل العميد.

My teacher explains everything in class. ٧

سَألَتنا المُدَرِّسة عن كلّ شيء في الفصل.

سَألتُ العميد والمُدَرِّسة عن الدروس في الفصل.

تَشرَح مُدَرِّستي كلّ شيء في الفصل.

Now answer these questions about Mario.

1. When does Mario start his day?

2. What does Mario always have by his side?

3. What does Dr. Zeinab like to do as she explains things in class?

4. What are the two landmarks near the institute?

5. Where does Mario eat lunch?

6. What does he usually order there?

7. How does Mario spend his evenings?

Page and screen الصَّفحة والشاشة

page	صَفحة/صَفحات
screen	شاشة/شاشات
comma	فَاصلة/فَاصلات
full stop	نُقطة/نُقَط
semicolon	فَاصلة مَنقوطة
question mark	عَلامة الاِستِفهام/عَلامات الاِستِفهام
exclamation mark	عَلامة التَّعَجُّب/عَلامات التَّعَجُّب
margin	هامِش/هَوامِش
sentence	جُملة/جُمَل
phrase	تَعبير/تَعبيرات
remark	مُلاحَظة/مُلاحَظات
password	كَلِمة المُرور/كَلِمات المُرور
attachments	مُرفَقات
applications	تَطبيقات
breakthrough	اِختِراق/اِختِراقات
genius (person)	عَبقَرِيّ/عَباقِرة
organized	مُنَظَّم/مُنَظَّمون
chemistry lab	مَعمَل الكيمياء
practical experiments	تَجارُب عَمَلِيَّة

Handy extras

noticeable progress	تَقَدُّم مَلحوظ
positive thoughts	أفكار إيجابيّة
negative behavior	سُلوك سَلبيّ
curious mind	عَقل فُضوليّ/عُقول فُضوليّة
Her writing style is clear and flowing.	أُسلوبها في الكِتابة واضِح وسَلِس.
The sequence of events is not logical.	تَسَلسُل الأحداث غير مَنطِقيّ.

EXERCISE
6·9

The school secretary's notes got muddled as she was writing two letters to Mr. Abulnoor about his two sons, Mounir and Hussein. Mounir is a star A student, while Hussein teeters on the outermost peripheries of education. Can you help her decide which notes belong to which letter?

عزيزي السيّد أبو النور،

تحية طيّبة،

إنجازات ابنكُم مُذهِلة يا سيّد أبو النور. (منير/حسين)

يا سيّد أبو النور، إنّنا نَبحَث عن حلّ لبعض مُشكِلات ابنكُم. (منير/حسين)

إن تَركِيزَه ليس هنا، ولكن في مكان آخر بعيد. (منير/حسين)

إنّه طَموح، ويحبّ المدرسة ويريد أن ينجَح. (منير/حسين)

إنّه يرفُض المشاركة، ولا يريد أن يَتَعَلَّم كيف يُغَيِّر أسلوبه السلبيّ. (منير/حسين)

إنّه يُناقِش ويسأل وله عَقل فُضوليّ. أسئلَته عميقة وأسلوبه جذّاب وناعِم. (منير/حسين)

إنّه يكرَه الفصل، ويريد أن يكون في الشُّرفة أو الشارِع أو على السُّلَّم أو بجوار المدخل. (منير/حسين)

إنه يُثَرثِر باستِمرار، ولِسانه طويل ولا يُرَكِّز في الحِصَص. (منير/حسين)

إنه يسير في طريق له اتِّجاه واحد: النجاح والجامعات الكبيرة. (منير/حسين)

إنه يَتّجِه نحو الرُّسوب. لا يمكن أن يَستَمِرّ معنا لأنّه يُضَيِّع وقته ووقتنا. (منير/حسين)

مع تَحِيات إدارة المدرسة،

سكرتير عامّ المدرسة

It's action time

to correct	صَحَّح/يُصَحِّح
to cross out	شَطَب/يَشْطُب
to delete	حَذَف/يَحذِف
to condense	اِختَصَر/يَختَصِر
to Arabize	عَرَّب/يُعَرِّب
to continue	اِستَمَرّ/يَستَمِرّ
to edit	حَرَّر/يُحَرِّر
to borrow	اِستَلَف/يَستَلِف
to punish	عاقَب/يُعاقِب
to cheat	غَشّ/يَغِشّ
to notice	لاحَظ/يُلاحِظ

Local flavors

ink on paper (implication: not worth much!)	حِبر على وَرَق
line, handwriting, calligraphy	خَطّ/خُطوط

Note that in addition to normal handwriting and stylized calligraphic writing, this word for "line" is also used in various combinations. Here are some examples:

railroad	خَطّ السِّكّة الحَديد
airline	خَطّ الطَّيران
telephone line	خَطّ الهاتِف
front line	خَطّ أَماميّ
power line, electricity	خَطّ الكَهرَباء
route	خَطّ السَّير
longitude	خَطّ الطول
latitude	خَطّ العَرض
equator	خَطّ الاِستِواء

Handy extras

Well done!	أَحسَنت!
Amazing!	مُدهِش!
Excellent!	مُمتاز!
It is very clear.	إنّه واضِح جِدّاً.
You are wrong.	أَنت مُخطِئ.
This is the right answer.	هذه هي الإجابة الصَحيحة.
sign language	لُغة الإشارة

Select the most reasonable ending to the following sentences.

١ وَرَقة الامْتِحان بيضاء! أين إجاباتك؟ واضِح جِدّاً أنّك ...

(تَجمَع التَبَرُّعات/لَم تُذاكِر/تَدرُس التاريخ)

٢ لا تَنسوا أن تَضَعوا عَلامة الاستِفهام بعد ...

(الاسم/السُّؤال/الإفطار)

٣ دَرَجاته تَتَزَلّق من سيِّء إلى أَسوأ وأَصبَحَ ...

(مُشكِلة في الفصل/مِلْء إبريق/فاصِلة مَنقوطة)

٤ سَأَشرَح لَكُم كلّ شيء في الفصل وأَنتُم ...

(تَغسِلون الجَزَر/على وشك الخُروج/تُراجِعون في البيت)

٥ أَخَذَت ابنَتكُم الدَرَجات النّهائية في كلّ شيء! إنّها ...

(لا تُرَكِّز في الحِصَص!/طالبة مُمتازة!/لا تُفيد المُجتَمَع!)

٦ امتِحان اللغة العربيّة سَهل ولكنّه طويل لأنّه ...

(استَمَرّ أربع ساعات/يوم الأربِعاء القادم/ما عدا يوم الجمعة)

٧ لا تُؤَجِّل عَمَل اليوم إلى ...

(الأمس/القرن الماضي/الغَدّ)

You have found some of Mrs. Dorothy Mayflower's classroom notes on her desk. Unable to resist, you have a quick peek.

Monday: Summarize chapter three, *Tale of Two Cities*.

Zakareya: Excellent! Writing style clear and flowing.

Mounir: No writing in the margins. Teacher only!

Tuesday: *Julius Caesar*, Act 1, Scene Two.

Wednesday: Explain synonyms. Questions/Answers.

Selim: Standards slipping. Additional tuition?

Nadia H: Learn when to use comma/semicolon.

Nadia R: Must solve problem of too much crossing out on page.

Rasheed: Problems at home?

Thursday: Revise for next week's examination.

Now, select the correct sentence.

١ يَدرُس فصل مسز مايفلاور "روميو وجولييت" هذه السنة.

مسز دوروثي مايفلاور هي مُدرِّسة اللّغة العربيّة والكيمياء.

يَدرُس فصل مسز مايفلاور شكسبير وديكنز هذه السنة.

٢ أُسلوب زكريا في الكتابة بالانجليزيّة ضعيف وسلبيّ.

أُسلوب زكريا في الكتابة بالانجليزيّة ممتاز لأنه واضح وسَلِس.

أُسلوب زكريا مثل أسلوب نادية رمزي ونادية حسن.

٣ لا تُريد مسز مايفلاور أن يَكتُب منير في الهامِش.

تُريد مسز مايفلاور من منير أن يَكتُب مثل نادية رمزي.

يُريد منير أن يَسألَ مسز مايفلاور عن أَساليب الكتابة.

٤ سليم طالب مُمتاز، ولكن مسز مايفلاور لم تُصَحِّح وَرَقَته.

مسز مايفلاور ترى أن سليم يَحتاج إلى دُروس إضافيّة.

سليم عنده قلم رَصاص أخضر قديم ولا يحتاج إلى قلم آخر.

٥ يدرس فصل مسز مايفلاور "يوليوس قيصر" يوم الثلاثاء.

يدرس فصل مسز مايفلاور "قصّة مدينتَين" يوم الثلاثاء.

يدرس فصل مسز مايفلاور "ماكبث" و"هاملت" هذه السنة.

٦ أُسلوب نادية رمزي مثل أُسلوب شكسبير وديكنز.

نادية رمزي تَشطُب كلمات كثيرة على الصفحة.

نادية حسن تَشطُب كلمات كثيرة على الصفحة.

٧ تريد مسز مايفلاور من الفصل أن يُلَخِّص ديكنز يوم الإثنين.

تريد مسز مايفلاور من الفصل أن يُلَخِّص شكسبير يوم الإثنين.

تريد مسز مايفلاور من الفصل أن يَشطُب كلمات كثيرة يوم الإثنين.

٨ تَرى مسز مايفلاور أن رشيد عنده بعض المشاكل في البيت.

تُريد مسز مايفلاور من رشيد أن يَكتُب مثل منير وزكريا.

تَرى مسز مايفلاور أن رشيد لا يحتاج إلى قلم آخر لونه أحمر.

٩ يَدرُس فصل مسز مايفلاور بعض الملاحظات يوم الأربعاء.

يَدرُس فصل مسز مايفلاور المُرادِفات يوم الأربعاء.

يَدرُس فصل مسز مايفلاور أُسلوب زكريا يوم الأربعاء.

١٠ يوم الثلاثاء هو يوم المُراجَعة لأن الإمتِحان يوم الأربعاء القادم.

يوم الإثنين هو يوم شكسبير لأنّنا لا نَحتاج إلى أكثر من أسبوع.

يوم الخميس هو يوم المُراجَعة لأن الإمتِحان في الأسبوع القادم.

Traveling and exploring
الجُزء السابِع: السَّفَر والاِستِكشاف

In this section we will look at the various sides of travel. In the Middle East we usually say that travel has seven benefits: السَّفَر لَهُ سَبعة فَوائِد. I couldn't tell you specifically what these seven benefits are, but generally speaking, we believe that to become a well rounded person, you need to have been around. Also, the number seven has a special ring to it unlike, say, six or eight.

Continents and regions القارّات والمَناطِق

Asia	آسيا
Africa	إفريقيا
Europe	أُوروبّا
North America	أَمريكا الشَّماليّة
South America	أَمريكا الجَنوبيّة
Australasia	قارّة أُستراليا
Antartica	القارّة القُطبيّة الجَنوبيّة
The Arctic	القُطب الشَّماليّ
The Middle East	الشَّرق الأَوسَط
The Far East	الشَّرق الأَقصَى
Central America	أَمريكا الوُسطى

Countries الدُّوَل

These are usually quite recognizable. Here are some countries that you may be able to recognize immediately because they sound almost identical in English and Arabic:

Iran, Pakistan, Afghanistan, Libya, Oman, Qatar, Canada, Thailand, Kenya, Ethiopia, Togo, Venezuela, Colombia

إيران، باكِستان، أَفغانِستان، ليبيا، عُمان، قَطَر، كَنَدا، تايلاند، كينيا، إثيوبيا، توجو، فنزويلا كولومبيا

Here are some countries that should sound familiar to you, but start with 'al-' (*the*):

Sudan, Kuwait, Denmark, Bahrain, Brazil, Yemen, Portugal

السّودان، الكُويت، الدِّنمارك، البَحرَين، البَرازيل، اليَمَن، البُرتُغال

These countries should sound familiar enough for you to have a good guess:

Argentina, Sweden, Finland, Tunisia, Lebanon, Syria, Mexico, Iraq, France, Italy, Spain

الأرجنتين، السويد، فنلَندا، تونس، لُبنان، سوريا، المَكسيك، العِراق، فَرَنسا، إيطاليا، إسبانيا

These countries sound different in English and Arabic:

Egypt, Jordan, United Arab Emirates, Great Britain, Saudi Arabia, Morocco, Japan, Algeria, Switzerland, United States, Germany, Greece, India, China, South Africa

مصر، الأُرُنّ، الإمارات، بريطانيا العُظمى، السَّعوديّة، المَغرِب، اليابان، الجَزائِر، سويسرا، الولايات المُتَّحِدة، أَلمانيا، اليونان، الهند، الصين، جَنوب إفريقيا

EXERCISE 7·1

In each group of three countries, two are in the same continent. Circle the odd one out.

١ باكستان، سويسرا، الهند

٢ السودان، فنزويلا، جنوب إفريقيا

٣ كولومبيا، فرنسا، الأرجنتين

٤ تايلاند، كينيا، إثيوبيا

٥ إيطاليا، فنلندا، تونس

٦ مصر، الصين، اليمن

٧ السعوديّة، توجو، ليبيا

٨ السويد، الولايات المُتَّحِدة، كندا

٩ أفغانستان، المغرب، الأردن

١٠ اليابان، اليونان، إيران

A few capital cities بَعض العَواصِم (عاصِمة/عَواصِم)

Paris, Madrid, London, Berlin, Lisbon, Athens, Rome, Riyadh, Cairo, Damascus, Abu Dhabi	باريس، مَدريد، لَنْدَن، بَرلين، لِشبونة، أَثينا، روما، الرِّياض، القاهِرة، دِمَشق، أَبو ظَبي
Doha, Beijing, Tokyo, Washington DC, Dublin, Muscat, Amman, Baghdad, Tehran, Warsaw	الدوحة، بِكين، طوكيو، واشِنطُن، دَبلِن، مَسقَط، عَمَّان، بَغداد، طَهران، وارسو
Caracas, Beirut, Manila, Nairobi, Oslo, Ankara, Khartoum, Jakarta, Sana'a, Stockholm	كاراكاس، بَيروت، مانيلَا، نيروبي، أوسلو، أَنقرة، الخَرطوم، جاكارتا، صَنعاء، ستوكهولم

Pretravel formalities إجراءات قَبل السَّفَر

procedure	إجراء/إجراءات
travel	سَفَر/أَسفار
ambassador	سَفير/سُفراء
embassy	سِفارة/سِفارات
consul	قُنصُل/قَناصِل
consulate	قُنصُليّة/قُنصُليّات
consular fees	مَصروفات قُنصُليّة
entry visa	تأشيرة دُخول/تأشيرات دُخول
passport	جَواز سَفَر/جَوازات سَفَر
date of issue	تاريخ الإصدار
expiry date	تاريخ الانتِهاء
validity	الصَلاحِيّة
reservation	حَجز/حُجوزات

It's action time

to issue	أَصدَر/يُصدِر
to stamp	أَشَّر/يُؤَشِّر
to expire (a term)	إنتَهى/يَنتَهي
to fill out (a form)	مَلأ/يَملأ
to repeat	كَرَّر/يُكَرِّر
to accept	قَبِل/يَقبَل
to reject	رَفَض/يَرفُض
to prepare	جَهَّز/يُجَهِّز
to send	أَرسَل/يُرسِل
to reserve	حَجَز/يَحجِز

Local flavors

Emir	أَمير/أُمَراء
Sultan	سُلطان/سَلاطين
emirate	إمارة، إمارات
sultanate	سَلطَنة، سَلطَنات
al-Bahrain means "the two seas"	البَحرين

Handy extras

Our embassy is located in the capital.	سِفارتُنا مَوجودة في العاصِمة.
You can fill out the form online.	يُمكِنك أن تَملأ الاستِمارة على الإنترنت.
You will need three recent photographs.	سَتَحتاج إلى ثَلاث صُوَر حَديثة.
It is valid for one visit only.	إنَّها صالِحة لِزيارة واحِدة فَقَط.
My visa is valid for six months from now.	تأشيرتي صالِحة لِمُدَّة سِتّة شُهور من الآن.
I need a multiple entry visa.	أحتاج إلى تأشيرة دُخول مُتَكَرِّر.
We're sorry, but your application has been refused.	نحن نَأسَف، ولكن طَلبك مَرفوض.
It will be ready after four working days.	سَتَكون جاهِزة بعد أربعة أيَّام عَمَل.

EXERCISE 7·2

Complete the sentences by choosing the right capital city.

١ سفارة كينيا في فرنسا موجودة في مدينة ـ_____ (مانيلّا، أنقرة، باريس)

٢ سفير الهند في العراق موجود في مدينة ـ_____ (طهران، بغداد، وارسو)

٣ سفارة باكِستان في قطر موجودة في مدينة ـ_____ (أبو ظبي، مسقط، الدوحة)

٤ سفير الصّين في السَعوديّة موجود في مدينة ـ_____ (كاراكاس، الرياض، عمّان)

٥ سفارة إيطاليا في مصر موجودة في مدينة ـ_____ (روما، دبلن، القاهرة)

٦ سفير الولايات المتّحدة في اليونان موجود في مدينة ـ_____ (أثينا، دمشق، ستوكهولم)

٧ سفارة كولومبيا في بريطانيا العظمى موجودة في مدينة ـ_____ (لشبونة، مدريد، لندن)

Handy extras

Is the capital the largest city in the country?	هل العاصِمة هي أكبر مدينة في الدَّولة؟
I live in the capital.	أُقيم في العاصِمة.
Does this mean I will need another visa?	هِل هذا مَعناه أنَّني سأحتاج إلى تأشيرة أخرى؟

Our plane will not land in the capital.	طائِرَتنا لَن تَهبِط في العاصمة.
They will fly directly to Oregon.	سَيطيرون مُباشَرةً إلى أوريجون.
My passport is in this bag.	جَواز سَفَري موجود في هذه الحقيبة.

EXERCISE 7·3

Help Ahmad tell us about his trip by selecting the appropriate words.

واشنطن/عَمّتي/باريس/طائرة/بغداد/الاستمارة/المكسيك/تأشيرة/عراقي/الولايات المتحدة/صالحة

١ أنا اسمي أحمد. أنا عِراقيٌّ وأُقيم في مدينة _____ وهي عاصِمتنا.

٢ جَواز سفري _____، وأنا سأُسافِر إلى _____ لزيارة عَمّتي في وِلاية فلوريدا.

٣ مَلأْتُ _____ وأرسَلتُها إلى السفارة.

٤ تأشيرَتي _____ لزيارة واحدة فقط.

٥ سَتَتَوَقَّف طائِرَتي في _____ عاصمة فرنسا لمُدّة ثلاث ساعات.

٦ بعد ذلك سَنَطير مُباشَرةً إلى _____ عاصمة الولايات المتّحدة.

٧ ومن هناك سآخُذ _____ أصغر إلى ميامي لأن _____ تعيش فيها.

٨ تُريد عَمّتي أن تأخُذني إلى أكابولكو في _____ ولكن هذا مَعناه أنّني سأحتاج إلى _____ أُخرى!

It's action time

to pay	دَفَع/يَدفَع
to take off	أقْلَع/يُقلِع
to land	هَبَط/يَهبِط
to check in, to register	سَجَّل/يُسَجِّل
to move	تَحَرَّك/يَتَحَرَّك
to stop	تَوَقَّف/يَتَوَقَّف
to fasten	رَبَط/يَربِط

More about travel المَزيد عَن السَّفَر

ship	سَفينة/سُفُن
seaport	ميناء/مَوانِئ
station	مَحَطّة/مَحَطّات

bus	باص/باصات
train	قِطار/قِطارات
return ticket	تَذْكَرة ذَهاب وعَودة/تَذاكِر ذَهاب وعَودة
seat	مَقْعَد/مَقاعِد
aisle	مَمَرّ/مَمَرّات
cabin	قَمرة/قَمرات
sleeper carriage	عَربة نَوم/عَربات نَوم
vaccination	تَطعيم/تَطعيمات

EXERCISE 7·4

Select the appropriate ending to create a meaningful sentence and write it down on the line provided.

في خمس محطّات/في وسط العاصمة/في ميناء مَرسيليا/بجوار الشبّاك/صالحة لمُدّة ستّة شهور/ لِتَزوروا ولاية كاليفورنيا

١ أريد أن أرى الضّواحي والحدائق، فحجزتُ مقعدي ــــــــــــــــ

٢ هذا ليس القطار المُباشِر، سَيَتَوَقَّف هذا القطار ــــــــــــــــ

٣ نستطيع أن نُؤَجِّل السفر قليلاً لأنّنا حصلنا على تأشيرة ــــــــــــــــ

٤ خُذوا الطائرة إلى سان فرنسيسكو أو لوس انجيلوس ــــــــــــــــ

٥ البَحّارة يحبّون فرنسا وسيتركُون السفينة لثلاثة أَيّام ــــــــــــــــ

٦ قُنصُلِيّة كوريا موجودة في الضواحي، ولكن السفارة ــــــــــــــــ

Sky and sea سَماء وبَحَر

departure gate	بَوّابة الخُروج/بَوّابات الخُروج
arrival hall	صالة الوُصول/صالات الوُصول
board	لَوحة/لَوحات
flight number	رَقم الرِّحلة/أرقام الرِّحَلات
boarding pass	بِطاقة الصُّعود/بِطاقات الصُّعود
first class	الدَّرَجة الأُولى
tourist class	الدَّرَجة السّياحيّة
pilot	قائِد الطائرة/قادة الطائرات

navigator	مَلّاح / مَلّاحون
flight attendant (m.)	مُضيف / مُضيفون
flight attendant (f.)	مُضيفة / مُضيفات
seat belt	حِزام الأمان / أحزِمة الأمان
duty free shop	الأسواق الحُرّة
security officer	ضابِط الأمن / ضُبّاط الأمن
passenger	راكِب / رُكّاب
quay	رَصيف / أرصِفة
ocean liner	عابِرة المُحيط / عابِرات المُحيط
(ship's) captain	قُبطان / قَباطِنة
luggage	حَقائِب
sailor	بَحّار / بَحّارة
lifeboat	زَوْرَق النَّجاة / زَوارِق النَّجاة
lifejacket	سُترة النَّجاة / سُترات النَّجاة

Handy extras

customs duty	رُسوم الجُمرُك / رُسوم الجَمارك
This is the passenger ship registered in Panama.	هذه هي سفينة الرُكّاب المُسَجَّلة في بنما.
First class seats are wider.	مَقاعِد الدرجة الأولى أعرَض.
The train fares are quite reasonable.	أسعار تَذاكِر القطارات مَعقولة جدّاً.
The security and customs officers took it away from him.	ضُبّاط الأمن والجَمارك أخَذوها منه.
The duty free bags you're carrying appear to be very heavy.	أكياس الأسواق الحُرّة التي تَحمِلها تبدو ثقيلة جدّاً.
My cabin has a porthole, but I'm not allowed to open it.	قَمَرتي لها شبّاك، ولكن مَمنوع عليَّ أن أفتَحهُ.
The trip will take three hours.	سَتَستغرِق الرِّحلة ثلاث ساعات.

EXERCISE 7·5

Select the correct word and write it in the space provided.

١ مَقاعِد الدرجة الأولى على الطائرات ــــــــــــ (ثقيلة/عريضة/للحقائب فقط)

٢ الطائرة ستهبُط في ــــــــــــ (الحقيبة/المطعم/المطار)

٣ الرُكّاب والبَحّارة يَنتَظِرون السفينة على رصيف ــــــــــــ (الميناء/السوق الحرّة/المحطّة)

٤ قال قائد الطائرة «أربُطوا أحزِمة الأمان لأنّنا» _____ (سنَتَناوَل العشاء/سنَغسِل الفاكهة/سنُقلِع)

٥ عندها مشكلة في جواز السفر فطلبَت المُساعَدة من _____ (القُنصُليّة/المُمَرِّضات/رِجال الأعمال)

٦ ضُبّاط الأمن طلبوا من الركّاب أن يفتحوا _____ (حقائبهم/بوّابات الخروج/سفارة بنما)

الـمُنتَجَع والـفُندُق Resort and hotel

الاستقبال	reception
نِصف إقامة	half board
إقامة كامِلة	full board
إفطار	breakfast
دَليل سِياحيّ	tour guide
سائِح/سُوّاح	tourist
سَرير أطفال/أسِرّة أطفال	crib
سَرير إضافيّ/أسِرّة إضافيّة	extra bed
جَناح/أجنِحة	suite
شاطِئ/شَواطِئ	beach
صالة رِياضة/صالات رِياضة	gymnasium
مَلعَب جولف/مَلاعِب جولف	golf course
مَلعَب تنس/مَلاعِب تنس	tennis court

EXERCISE

7·6

Put the following sentences in the correct chronological order. (Clue: belts to beds!)

١ ذهبنا إلى المطعم لتَناوُل العشاء.

٢ أخذنا باص سياحيّ من المطار إلى الفندق.

٣ أخذنا حقائِبنا إلى الغُرَف.

٤ ربطنا أحزِمة الأمان استِعداداً للهُبوط.

٥ هبطَت بنا الطائرة في المطار.

٦ مشينا في حدائق المُنتَجَع بعد الأكل.

٧ رجعنا إلى الغرف لننام.

٨ ملأنا الاستِمارات في قِسم الاستِقبال.

Handy extras

Do I need a vaccination against malaria?	هل أَحتاج إلى تَطعيم ضِدّ الملاريا؟
We will get the tourist visa at the airport.	سَنَحصُل على التأشيرة السِّياحِيّة من المَطار.
The health club is next to the nightclub.	النادي الصِحّيّ بِجوار المَلهى اللَّيلِيّ.
Do we pay in the local currency?	هل نَدفَع بالعُملة المَحَلِّيّة؟

غُرفة: حُجرة Note these two words both mean "room," and you are likely to come across them in equal measure. However, I believe one of them has become slightly more "glamorous" than the other because it has been adopted by the modern hotel industry in the Arab world. In a hotel context, you are therefore more likely to find:

room number	رَقَم الغُرفة/أَرقام الغُرَف
room key	مِفتاح الغُرفة/مَفاتيح الغُرَف
room service	خِدمة الغُرَف

Camping and wilderness التَخييم والخَلاء

desert	صَحراء/صَحارى
oasis	واحة/واحات
dune	كَثيب/كُثبان
star	نَجم/نُجوم
(water) spring	عَين ماء/عُيون ماء
(water) well	بِئر/آبار
quicksand	رِمال ناعمة
hill	تَلّ/تِلال
beduin	بَدوي/بَدو
guide	دَليل/أَدِلّاء
track (road)	مِدَقّ/مِدَقّات
asphalt	أَسفَلت
campsite	مُعَسكَر/مُعَسكَرات
tent	خَيمة/خِيام
mallet	مِطرَقة خَشَبِيّة/مَطارِق خَشَبِيّة
fire	نار
firewood	حَطَب
a grill	شَوّاية/شَوّايات
trap	مَصيَدة/مَصائِد
rope	حَبل/جِبال

map	خَريطة/خَرائِط
compass	بوصلة/بوصلات
cacti	صَبّار
scorpion	عَقرَب/عَقارِب

EXERCISE
7·7

Select the correct word and write it in the space provided.

أخذنا الطائرة ــــــــــ (لنَأكل/لنملأ الاستِمارة/لنطير) إلى ــــــــــ (فنلندا/مصر/ألاسكا) لِنَقضي إجَازتنا في الصَّحراء. أخذنا مَعنا ــــــــــ (الخِيام/الأحزِمة/الأرصِفة) لِنَنام فيها. رَكِبنا سيّارة خاصّة اتّجهنا إلى أعماق الصحراء. قُدنا سيّارَتنا فوق ــــــــــ (التّلال/الشجر/النُّجوم) وبين ــــــــــ (مَطاعِم السمك/الأسواق الحُرّة/كُثبان الرِّمال) لمُدّة تسع ساعات إلى أن وَصَلنا إلى ــــــــــ (سِفارة كندا/الواحة/الصالة الرِّياضيّة)، هناك نَصَبنا ــــــــــ (الحدائِق/الخِيام/ مَلاعِب التنس) ونِمنا حتّى الصباح. قَضينا خمسة أيّام رائِعة، رَكِبنا ــــــــــ (الجِمال/المَطارق الخشبيّة/أحزِمة الأمان) بالنَّهار، وفي الليل جَلَسنا حول ــــــــــ (العَقارِب/الحقائِب/النار) نُغَنّي ونَتَكَلَّم ونَضحَك ونَنظُر إلى ــــــــــ (الآبار/المُضيفات/النُّجوم) اللامِعة في السماء. كانَت رحلة رائِعة!

EXERCISE
7·8

Vacations could go either way. Read the following sentences, then write down whether they represent رائِع خبَر *(Great news!) or* سَيِّء خبَر *(Bad news!).*

١ مَقاعدكُم في الدَرَجة السِّياحيّة مَشغولة. سَنُعطيكُم المَقاعِد الموجودة في الدرجة الأولى. ــــــــــ

٢ يَبدو أنّنا نَسينا قُبطان السفينة وبعض البَحّارة على رصيف المِيناء. ــــــــــ

٣ سَيَصِل القطار في مَوعِده. ــــــــــ

٤ أُنظُر إلى اللّوحة! نصف الرحلات مُتأخِّرة والنصف الثاني أُلغِيَت! ــــــــــ

٥ عَمّتي سَقَطَت من فوق الجمل على نَبات الصَّبّار قبل أن يَلدَغها العَقرَب. ــــــــــ

٦ السَّيّدة البَدويّة أعطَتني هذا الحَلَق كهَديّة لي والعُقد كهَديّة لابنتي. ــــــــــ

Khalil went on a "once-in-a-lifetime cruise" last week. Read his postcard to his friend Samir.

عزيزي سمير،

أمس، نزلتُ من السفينة وأخذتُ جولة لزيارة المَعالِم. عُدتُ إلى الميناء لأكتَشِف أن سفينَتنا اختَفَت. قُبطان السفينة أبحَرَ ونَسى بعض الركّاب والبحّارة على رصيف الميناء. سفينتي اختَفَت ومعها حقائبي! عُدتُ إلى وسط المدينة لأبحَث عن فندق. اقترَبَت منّي فتاة طويلة، خفيفة الدم، تَبدو ثَريّة، ومَلامِحها جذّابة. سأَلَتني إن كُنتُ أريد المُساعَدة. جَلَسنا وشَرِبنا فنجان شاي وثَرثَرنا قليلاً. كان معي حقيبة صغيرة فيها جواز سفري وتليفوني وبعض الدولارات. ذَهَبتُ إلى الحَمّام، وعُدتُ لأكتَشِف أن هذه الفتاة ليسَت فقط خفيفة الدم، ولكنّها خفيفة اليد أيضاً! اختَفَت الفتاة، وحقيبتي الصغيرة اختَفَت معها. نحن الآن في مُنتَصَف الليل. أنا أجلس الآن على رصيف شارع كبير. أصابِعي تَـجَمَّدَت. أنفي تَـجَمَّدَ. لم آكُل شيئاً منذ أن تَناوَلتُ الإفطار أمس سَوى نصف عود كَرَفس وَجَدتُه في كوب على مائدة أحد المطاعم على الرصيف. طَلَبتُ المُساعَدة من القُنصُليّة. قالوا إن هناك بعض الإجراءات لأنّني بلا جواز سفر. القُنصُليّة ستُعِدّ لي تَذكِرة طائرة للعَودة فقط. سأعود بهذه التذكِرة مُباشَرةً إلى بَلَدنا، ولكنّها سَتَكون جاهِزة بعد أربعة أيّام عمل.

مع تَـحِياتي،

خليل.

EXERCISE
7·9

Select the English that best represents the Arabic.

١ ذهبتُ في جولة لزيارة المَعالِم.

I am planning to see all my friends.

I saw some famous people yesterday.

I went on a tour to visit the sites.

٢ سفينتنا اختَفَت ومعها حقائبنا.

Our ship and our guide have both disappeared.

Our ship has docked and we'll go on a tour.

Our ship has disappeared with our suitcases.

٣ اقترَبَت منّي فتاة جذّابة.

An attractive girl approached me.

I was distracted by a beautiful girl.

We are nearer to the end of the line.

٤ أخذَت جواز سَفري وتليفوني وبعض الدولارات.

She told me this phone would cost a few dollars.

She returned my passport, but kept all the dollars.

She took my passport, my phone, and some dollars.

٥ أجلس الآن على رصيف شارع كبير.

I am now sitting on the sidewalk of a big street.

I am now standing on the corner of a big street.

I am now alone at my table just watching people.

٦ لم آكل شيئاً سوى نصف عود كرفس.

My favorite soup has always been cream of celery.

I haven't eaten anything except half a celery stick.

I've eaten so much; I couldn't have half a celery stick.

EXERCISE

7·10

Add the missing words in the English translation to match the Arabic.

١ قُبطان السفينة أَبحَرَ.

The _____ of the ship has _____.

٢ مَلامِحها جَذّابة وخفيفة الظِّلّ.

Her _____ are _____ and she's funny.

٣ كانت خفيفة الظِّلّ، ولكنّها كانت خفيفة اليد أيضاً.

She _____ funny, but 'light of _____' too.

٤ أنا على الرصيف وأصابعي تَجَمَّدَت.

I'm on the _____ and my _____ are _____.

٥ طلبتُ المساعدة من القُنصُليّة.

I asked for _____ from the _____.

٦ ستَستَغرق الإجراءات أربعة أيّام عمل.

The _____ will take _____ working days.

Now answer these questions.

1. Why did Khalil leave the cruise ship?

2. Why did he return to the city center?

3. Describe the person who offered to help him.

4. What did Khalil keep in his little bag?

5. Where was Khalil sitting to write this postcard?

6. Describe the last thing he's eaten.

7. When does he expect to fly home?

Now, read Samir's postcard to Khalil. He's on a "once-in-a-lifetime desert safari."

عزيزي خليل،

اِبتَسَمَت لي المُضيفة وطَلَبَت مِنّي أن أجلس في أحد مَقاعِد الدرجة الأولى لأنَّ جميع مقاعد الدرجة السياحيّة على الطائرة محجوزة. مقاعد الدرجة الأولى عريضة وناعمة وطريّة، وكانت الوجبة مُمتازة! كنت أجلس بجوار النَّجمة السينمائيّة الجميلة فيفي أبو يوسف! ثَرثَرنا معاً طوال الرحلة وهي قالَت إنَّني خفيف الظلّ! وقبل الهبوط، طَلَبَت أن تَأتي معي في رِحلتي لِتَرى الصحراء معي! بيني وبينك، أنا وافَقتُ في أقَلّ من لحظة! المُنتَجع هنا مُدهِش، والمجموعة كلّها من نفس الجيل تقريباً. أنا الآن في خيمتي في الواحة، وفيفي في خيمتها لأنَّها تَأخذ ساعتَين كلّ يوم لِلإعداد للفيلم الجديد. هذه إجازة العُمر يا خليل! أنا وفيفي نَلعَب على التِّلال والكُثبان الرَملِيّة، ونَستَحِمّ في عُيون الماء ونركب الجمال، وفي آخر النهار نجلس حول النار لِنأكل وجبة مشويّة على الفَحم أو الخَشَب، وننظر إلى النُّجوم في السماء. الحياة هنا بسيطة ولكن أنا لا أريد أن أعود إلى بيتي أبداً!

مع تحياتي،

سمير

Select the English that best represents the Arabic.

١ اِبتَسَمَت لي النجمة الجذّابة وقالت، "أنت خفيف الظلّ!"

The movie star looked at me and said, "You're funny!"

The famous star looked at me and said, "I know you!"

The attractive star smiled at me and said, "You're funny!"

٢ المجموعة كلّها من نفس الجيل.

The whole group appears to be having fun.

The whole group are from the same generation.

Every generation appears to be having more fun.

٣ مَقاعِد الدرجة السياحيّة كلّها محجوزة فجلستُ في الدرجة الأولى.

All first class seats were reserved so I complained.

All tourist class passengers were complaining at once.

All tourist class seats were reserved so I sat in first class.

٤ طَلَبَت أن تأتي معي في رحلتي إلى الواحة.

She asked to come with me on my trip to the oasis.

They asked to come with me on my trip to the desert.

He asked me a few questions about my trip to the oasis.

٥ بيني وبينك، أنا وافَقتُ في أقلّ من لحظة!

Between you and me, I agreed in less than an instant!

Between you and me, she and I hated every minute of it!

Between you and him, I think I'd rather go with you!

٦ تأخذ فيفي ساعتَين كلّ يوم للإعداد لفيلمها.

Fifi's new movie is about two hours long but it's good.

Fifi is so busy, she makes about two movies a year.

Fifi takes two hours a day to prepare for her movie.

٧ نجلس حول النار لنأكل وجبة مشويّة.

We sit around the grill and wait for our meal.

We sit around the fire and grill our own meal.

We sit around the fire to eat a grilled meal.

Decide which sentences are true and which are false.

1. Samir used all his savings to buy a first class ticket for this flight. (T/F)

2. On the plane, Samir sat next to a beautiful movie star. (T/F)

3. The beautiful movie star thought Samir had no sense of humor whatsoever. (T/F)

4. Samir asked Fifi Abuyousif if she would like to join him on his desert safari. (T/F)

5. Most of the guests at the desert resort were of similar age. (T/F)

6. Fifi Abuyousif spent two hours every day preparing for her new film role. (T/F)

7. Fifi and Samir had separate tents, and enjoyed the resort's daytime activities together. (T/F)

8. Fifi and Samir ate evening meals that were grilled on either charcoal or wood. (T/F)

9. Samir can't wait to get back home. (T/F)

10. In a broad sense, Samir has been quite lucky on this trip. (T/F)

EXERCISE
7·14

Now, based on these two postcards, select the appropriate phrase to fit the gap.

١ شَرِبَ خليل ـــــــــــــــــــ مع الفتاة التي أخذَت حقيبته واختفَت.

(زجاجة كولا/فنجان شاي/عصير برتقال)

٢ عاد خليل إلى الميناء لِيَكتَشِف أن ـــــــــــــــــــ .

(السفينة اختفت/القبطان يبتسم/الميناء مُغلق يوم الجمعة)

٣ الفرق بين رحلة سمير ورحلة خليل هو ـــــــــــــــــــ جدّاً!

(فرق شاسِع/الأبيض والأسود/النهار والليل)

٤ النجمة الجميلة فيفي أبو يوسف قالت لخليل: أنت ـــــــــــــــــــ !

(ثقيل الدم/تُثَرثِر كثيراً!/خفيف الظلّ!)

٥ كان سمير يأكل حول النار وينظر إلى ـــــــــــــــــــ .

(طبق فيفي/النجوم في السماء/الأفلام القديمة)

٦ خليل قال لسمير "أنا لا أريد أن أعود إلى ـــــــــــــــــــ أبداً!"

(هذا المنتجع/هذه النجمة السينمائية/بيتي)

٧ بعض الناس يقولون أن السفر له ـــــــــــــــــــ .

(تسعة أشكال/خمسة ألوان/سبع فَوائِد)

Shopping and selecting
الجُزْء الثامِن: التَّسَوُّق والاِختِيار

Shopping and selecting
الجُزْء الثامِن: التَّسَوُّق والاِختِيار

I'm just looking: one . . . أَنا أَنظُر فَقَط: واحِد . . .

merchandise	بِضاعة/بَضائِع
women's clothing	مَلابِس حَريميّة
men's section	القِسم الرِجاليّ
garments	ثَوب/ثِياب
accessories	كَماليّات
suggestion	اِقتِراح/اِقتِراحات
decision	قَرار/قَرارات
customer service	خِدمة العُمَلاء
size	مَقاس/مَقاسات
ready-made	جاهِز
made-to-measure	تَفصيل
silk	حَرير/حَرائِر
cotton	قُطن/أَقْطان
flax linen	كَتَّان
wool	صوف/أَصواف
leather	جِلد/جُلود
original	أَصليّ
traditional	تَقليديّ
used	مُستَعمَل
local	مَحلّيّ
imported	مُستَورَد
antique	عَتيق
handmade	شُغل يَدويّ
embroidered	مُزَرْكَش
ribbed	مُضَلَّع

p

q

r

Handy extras

fashion show	عَرض أَزياء/عُروض أَزياء
It's in the shop window.	إنّها في واجهة المَحَلّ.
It suits me.	إنّها تُناسِبني.
It is not to my taste.	إنّها لا تُناسِب ذَوقي.
Maybe I'll take it.	رُبّما آخُذُها.
May I have a look around?	مُـمكِن آخُذ فِكرة؟

Literally, "looking around" is expressed as "taking an idea."

EXERCISE
8·1

Select the Arabic question that best represents the English.

Is this the right size for me? ١

هل هذا هو السِّعر المُناسِب لي؟

هل هي على اليمين بجوار المَدخَل؟

هل هذا هو المَقاس المُناسِب لي؟

Is this wool or cotton? ٢

هل المدير في مكتبه الآن؟

هل هذا صوف أَم قُطن؟

هل تُريدون القُطن المَحَلّيّ؟

Where is the men's section? ٣

هل هذا هو القِسم الرِجاليّ؟

أين القِسم الرِّجالية؟

هل تَعرفون هذا الرَّجُل؟

Is this local leather? ٤

هل هذا جِلد مَحَلّيّ؟

هل هو جاهِز أَم تَفصيل؟

هل هذا الجِلد مُستَورَد؟

Do you have any suggestions? ٥

هل هذا الاِقتِراح مُناسِب؟

هل عندك اقتراحات؟

هل عندك ألوان أُخرى؟

Is this hijab silk and cotton? ٦

هل هذا الحِجاب من الحَرير المُستَورَد؟

هل هذا الحِجاب من الحَرير والقُطن؟

هل هذا الحِجاب من قِسم الكَماليّات؟

EXERCISE
8·2

Complete each of the following sentences by making the logical choice from the three options that follow it.

١ أحمد في القسم الرجاليّ لأنّه ــــــــــــــــــــ

رَجُل جَذّاب وكريم ويحبّ الاِبتِسام

يَحتاج إلى بعض الملابس الجديدة

يريد غسّالة ملابس جديدة ومكواة

٢ هذه البَضائِع من الصوف لأن ــــــــــــــــــــ

مَوسِم الشِّتاء اِقتَرَبَ

المحلّ مُغلَق يوم الجمعة

الحَلّة على نار هادِئة

٣ هذه البَضائِع أرخَص كثيراً لأنّها ــــــــــــــــــــ

جديدة

مُستَعمَلة

زَرقاء

٤ هذه البَضائِع أغلى كثيراً لأنّها ــــــــــــــــــــ

شُغل يَدويّ

تُناسِبني

بجوار الشُّباك

٥ ليس هذا الحِزام مَقاسي لأنّه _____

بدون ثَلج

هذا الأسبوع

كبير الحَجم

٦ إنّها في واجِهة المَحَلّ لأنّها _____

بضائع جديدة وجميلة وجذّابة

بَلّاعة قديمة وماسورة مُستَعمَلة

رَسَبَت في كلّ المَوادّ

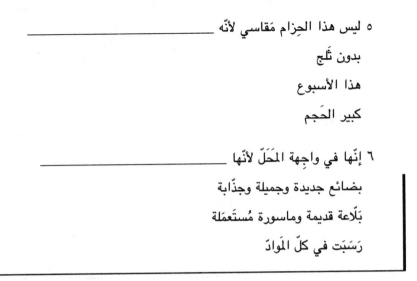

EXERCISE

8·3

Circle the odd one out.

١ شُغل يَدوي/مُزَركَش/عَرض أزياء

٢ ملابس أمّي/واجِهة المَحَلّ/حجاب أُختي

٣ قَرارات/مستعمل/عتيق

٤ مقاسي/دجاج مشوي/يناسبني

٥ عندي فكرة/عندي اقتراح/عندي سيارة

٦ قَهوتي/أصليّ/تقليديّ

I'm just looking: two . . .   أنا أَنظُر فَقَط: اِثنان

retailer	تاجِر التَّجزِئة/تُجّار التَّجزِئة
wholesaler	تاجِر الجُملة/تُجّار الجُملة
distributor	مُوَزِّع/مُوَزِّعون
agent	وَكيل/وُكَلاء
cost	تَكلِفة/تَكاليف
price	سِعر/أسعار؛ ثَمن/أَثمان
inexpensive	رَخيص
expensive	غالٍ
installment	قِسط/أقساط

down payment	دُفعة مُقَدَّمة/دُفعات مُقَدَّمة
opportunity	فُرصة/فُرَص
tempting offer	عَرض مُغرٍ/عُروض مُغرية
supply and demand	عَرض وطَلب
reasonable price	سِعر مَعقول
economic	اِقتِصاديّ
at least	عَلى الأَقَلّ
at most	عَلى الأكثَر
free sample	عَيّنة مَجّانيّة/عَيّنات مَجّانيّة
cost price	سِعر التَّكلِفة
raw materials	المادّة الخام/المَوادّ الخام
device, (television) set	جِهاز/أجهِزة
packaging	تَغليف
parcel	طَرد/طُرود
shipping	شَحن
delivery	تَوصيل
insurance	تَأمين
damage	تَلَف

EXERCISE

8·4

Match the opposites.

مُستَعمَل	١ على الأَقَلّ
مُستَورَد	٢ رَخيص
رجاليّ	٣ تُجّار التَّجزِئة
تفصيل	٤ محلّيّ
على الأكثَر	٥ حريميّ
غالٍ	٦ جاهز
تُجّار الجُملة	٧ جديد

Select the suitable Arabic sentence.

Yes, the price is reasonable, but I don't need a new shirt. ١

نعم، السعر جديد، ولكن القميص أيضاً جديد وهذا لا يُناسِبني.

نعم، السعر مَعقول، ولكن أنا لا أحتاج إلى قميص جديد.

نعم، القميص جديد، ولكن أنا لا أريد أن أدفع هذا السعر.

At the end of the season you will not find all the sizes. ٢

في النهاية، لم تَختَلِف المقاسات عن السنة الماضية.

بَحَثنا في كلّ مكان ولكن لم نَفهَم الأسباب الحقيقيّة.

في نهاية المَوسِم لن تَجِدوا كلّ المقاسات.

The agent wants a down payment before shipping. ٣

السفينة لها وَكيل في كلّ ميناء للشَّحن.

يريد الوكيل دُفعة مُقَدَّمة قبل الشَّحن.

يريد وكيل السفينة دُفعة مُقَدَّمة بعد التَّغليف.

Look at the damage! I bought it here last Thursday! ٤

تعالوا يوم الخميس! سنذهب معاً إلى بيت التاجر لنَسأَله.

أنظُروا إلى التَّلَف! أنا اِشتَرَيتُها هنا يوم الخميس الماضي!

سنذهب يوم الخميس! التَّلَف في كلّ مكان وهذا غير معقول!

What are the costs of packaging and delivery? ٥

ما هي أَساليب التَّأمين والتَّغليف؟

ما هي أسعار التَّأمين عند الوكيل؟

ما هي تَكاليف التَّغليف والتَّوصيل؟

If it is a free sample, I'll take ten. ٦

إن كانَت عَيِّنة مَجّانيّة، سآخُذ عشرة.

إن كانَت عشرة، خُذ خمسة واعطِني خمسة.

إن كانَت عَيِّنات مَجّانيّة، سآخُذ إجازة.

Read this dialog which takes place in a large mall.

منصور: "أريد أن أشتَري جهاز تليفزيون من فضلك."

البائِعة (تَبتَسِم): "عندنا اليوم عَرض مُغرٍ على حَقائِب السَّفَر. مثلاً نَبيع هذه الحقائب السَّوداء بِسعر الجُملة. ولكن يَجب أن تُسرع لأن هذا العَرض المُغري موجود لثلاثة شُهور فقط."

منصور: "أَشكُرك. أنا لا أريد حقيبة سَفَر. عندي في البيت تسع حقائب سفر. أنا أريد أن أشتري جهاز تليفزيون."

البائِعة (تبتسم): "هذا الأسبوع فقط، هناك فُرصة نادِرة لِشِراء هذه المَراوِح الزَّرقاء. إنّها اقتصاديّة ومَتينة وسعرها معقول جدّاً."

منصور: "في الحقيقة أنا عندي مراوح كثيرة في البيت. رُبَّما ثماني مَراوِح أو تِسَع. لا أَتَذَكَّر."

البائِعة (تبتسم): "هل تعرف أن هذا المحلّ هو الوكيل والمُوزِّع لِثَلّاجات "ايجلو بارك" المَشهورة؟ يُـمكِنك أن تَشتَري ثلّاجة "ايجلو بارك" اليوم بِسعر التَّكلِفة. وأيضاً التَّغليف والشَّحن والتَّوصيل والتَّأمين كلّها خِدمات مَجانيّة."

منصور: "ثلّاجات ايجلو بارك جميلة. أنا عندي واحدة في كلّ غرفة من بيتي. ولكن لماذا لا تريدين أن تَعطيني جهاز تليفزيون؟"

البائِعة: "هل تَرى هذا الرَّجُل الذي يَقِف هناك بجوار الباب؟ اِشتَرى هذا الرجل آخِر جهاز تليفزيون عندنا في المحلّ من خمس دَقائِق فقط."

منصور: "في الحقيقة أنا لا أَحتاج إلى جهاز تليفزيون آخِر اليوم. عندي تسعة في البيت وأربعة في المَخزَن فوق السَّطح. ماذا قُلتِ عن العرض على حقائب السفر السوداء؟"

EXERCISE
8·6

Decide if the sentences about the dialog are true or false.

1. The reduced price on suitcases is available for one week only. (T/F)

2. Mansour appears to be a compulsive buyer. (T/F)

3. The man by the door bought the last Igloo Park refrigerator. (T/F)

4. Mansour desperately needs a new television set today. (T/F)

5. The sales girl nearly always smiles. (T/F)

6. Delivery of a new Igloo Park refrigerator will cost extra. (T/F)

Now answer the questions.

1. Why did Mansour visit the department store?

2. How were the black suitcases priced?

3. What are the positive features of the blue fans?

4. How many television sets does Mansour own in total?

5. What appliance does Mansour have in every room?

6. When was the last television set sold?

Here are some phrases and sentences loosely based on the passage above. Select the Arabic that best represents the English.

It's a tempting offer! ١

إنّه جهاز جديد!

إنّه عرض مغرٍ!

إنّها حقيبة سفر!

We are selling these black suitcases. ٢

نريد هذه الحقائب السوداء.

نبيع هذه الحقائب السوداء.

نعرض هذه الأجهِزة اليوم.

the wholesale price ٣

سعر معقول

عرض سريع

سعر الجملة

You must hurry! ٤

يجب أن تُسرِع!

سعر معقول جداً!

هذا الجهاز سريع!

There's a rare opportunity. ٥

هناك حقائب نادرة.

هذه الأجهزة سوداء.

هناك فرصة نادرة.

I have one in every room. ٦

عندي واحدة في كلّ غرفة.

عندي غرفة في كلّ بيت.

عندي واحدة وأريد غرفة.

He bought the last set. ٧

سآخذ هذا الجهاز.

اِشتَرى آخر جهاز.

اِشتَرى جهازاً من هنا.

free services ٨

ثلاث خدمات

خدمات مجانيّة

ثلاث فُرَص

They are economic and famous. ٩

إنّها مشهورة ومتينة.

إنّها متينة واِقتِصاديّة.

إنّها اِقتِصاديّة ومشهورة.

Why don't you want to give me a suitcase? ١٠

لماذا لا تريدين أن تُعطيني فُرصة؟

هل تريد حقيبة زرقاء أم ثلّاجة بيضاء؟

لماذا لا تريدين أن تُعطيني حقيبة؟

Here are some sentences loosely based on the passage above. Select the English that best represents the Arabic.

١ عندنا اليوم عرض مغرٍ على أَجهِزة التليفزيون.

Yesterday we had a tempting offer on suitcases.

It's a nice television, but you must resist temptation.

We have a tempting offer on television sets today.

٢ إنّها فُرصة نادرة لشراء غسّالة.

It's a rare opportunity to buy a washing machine.

It's a rare washing machine that washes anything.

It's an opportunity to have a quick wash before we go.

٣ الحقائب البيضاء بسِعر الجُملة.

The wholesale price is not at all reasonable.

The blue suitcases are cheaper than the white.

The white suitcases are at the wholesale price.

٤ ربَّما ثماني مَراوِح أو تسع.

Maybe I'll buy nine fans.

I'll take eight fans today.

Maybe eight fans or nine.

٥ هذا الرجل هو الوكيل والمُوَزِّع.

This man distributes suitcases in the market.

This man is the agent and distributer.

This man buys a lot of fans every day.

٦ عندي تسعة في المَخزَن فوق السَّطح.

Our washing machine has nine new shirts.

I have nine in the warehouse on the roof.

Our roof has an old warehouse with a fan.

٧ ماذا قُلتِ عن هذه الحقائب الزرقاء؟

What did you say about these blue suitcases?

Who put the last blue fan in the other warehouse?

What did you say is the color of the blue suitcases?

Local flavors

market	سـوق/أَسواق
flea market	سوق الكانتو/أسواق الكانتو
closed for prayer	مُغلَق للصَّلاة
carpet	سَجَّادة/سَجاجيد
henna	حِنّاء
perfumer	عَطّار/عَطّارون
essence	خُلاصة/خُلاصات
rose oil	عِطر الوَرد
musk scent	رائِحة المِسك
ambergris	عِطر العنبَر
trade secret	سِرّ المِهنة/أَسرار المِهنة
cloak (abaya wrap)	عَباءة/عَبائات

And, just in case you need to use them both, "dagger" is خِنجَر/خَناجِر. And, while we're here, "poisoned" is مَسموم.

It's action time حان وقت الأفعال

to extract	إستَخرَج/يَستَخرِج
to blend	خَلَط/يَخلِط
to distill	قَطَّر/يُقَطِّر
to advertise	أَعلَن/يُعلِن
to embellish	زَخرَف/يُزَخرِف
to adorn	زَيَّن/يُزَيِّن
to assess (value)	ثَمَّن/يُثَمِّن
to guarantee	ضَمَن/يَضمَن
to haggle	ساوَم/يُساوِم
to convince	أَقنَع/يُقنِع
to copy	قَلَّد/يُقَلِّد

to confirm	أَكَّد/يُؤَكِّد
compare	قارَن/يُقارِن
to resemble	شابَه/يُشابِه
to choose	اِختار/يَختار
to decide	قَرَّر/يُقَرِّر
to pierce	خَرَم/يَخرُم
to dye	صَبَغ/يَصبِغ
to copy (fake; imitate)	قَلَّد/يُقَلِّد
to copy (a document)	نَسَخ/يَنسَخ

Brenda is visiting a traditional Middle Eastern market to do a profile of some local traders and craftsmen for a US television channel. Brenda and her interpreter start the interviews with Ahmed, who owns a traditional perfume store.

Brenda: "Tell us, Ahmed, how long have you been in the perfume business?"

أحمد: "نحن هنا في هذا السوق من حَوالي خمس وسبعين سنة."

Brenda: "That's a long time!"

أحمد: "نعم. المرحوم جَدّي كان أكبر وأَشهَر عَطّار في هذا السوق. اليوم، أنا عطّار، وأبي عَطّار، وعَمّي وأولاد عَمّي عَطّارون. في الحقيقة أُسرتي كلّها تعمل في العُطور."

Brenda: "I see. But, why do you think the business has lasted for such a long time?"

أحمد: "لماذا؟ لأنّكُم سَتَجِدون عندنا العطور الأصليّة فقط. نحن نَعرِف كيف نُقَطِّر ونَستَخرِج ونَخلِط الخُلاصات. إنّها أسرار المِهنة التي لا تَخرُج من هذا الباب."

Brenda: "Yes, but, when I look around, it is not exactly a cheap store!"

أحمد: "نعم. رُبّما كانت الأسعار عندنا غالية قليلاً ولا تُناسِب كلّ الناس. ولكن لا تَنسي أن اليوم، تَكلِفة المادّة الخام مُرتَفِعة جدّاً."

Brenda: "Is there a lot of competition?"

أحمد: "نعم. بعض التُّجّار يُحاوِلون أن يُقَلِّدونا. إنّهم يُزَيِّنون ويُزَخرِفون الزُّجاجات ويَضعونها في أكياس مُزَركِشة ولكن، في النِّهاية، هم يضعون العُطور المُقَلَّدة في الزجاجات."

Brenda: "Finally, what would your message be to our viewers in the United States if they were to come to your shop one day?"

أحمد: "أَهلاً وسَهلاً بِكُم في أيّ وَقت. عُطورنا الأصليّة لا تُقارَن. الأسعار موجودة على الزجاجات. نحن لا نُساوِم!"

Identify the English sentence that best represents the Arabic.

١ نحن نعرف كيف نُقَطِّر.

We know why it is there.

We know who uses them.

We know how to distill.

٢ أشهر عطّار في المدينة

the most famous perfume brands

we waited months for this perfume

the most famous perfumer in the city

٣ أُسرتي كلّها تعمل معي.

Their whole family knows about it.

My whole family works with me.

His whole family is in the business.

٤ إنّها أسرار المِهنة.

These are the trade secrets.

They are a secretive family.

We always keep our secrets.

٥ الأسعار لا تُناسِب كلّ الناس.

People say they will when they won't.

The prices don't suit everyone.

These people are not suitable.

٦ لا تنسي هذه الزجاجات.

Don't take the whole bottle.

Don't forget to take a bottle.

Don't forget these bottles.

٧ تَكلِفة المادّة الخام مُرتَفِعة.

The cost of the raw material is high.

It is high time we bought some new materials.

The bottle is on the high shelf in the back.

٨ أهلاً وسهلاً بكم في أيّ وقت.

Your time is up and we're closing now.

You are welcome to return tomorrow.

You are welcome any time.

٩ نحن لا نُساوِم.

Sorry, we are closed.

We don't need any.

We don't haggle.

١٠ إنّهم يُزَيِّنون ويُزَخرِفون.

We use the essence of wild flowers and seeds.

We distill and bottle it ourselves.

They adorn and embellish.

EXERCISE
8·11

Identify the Arabic expressions in Brenda's interview that best represent the following, then write them down in the space provided.

1. my late grandfather _____

2. the most famous perfumer _____

3. around seventy five _____

4. in fact, my entire family _____

5. a little expensive _____

6. but, in the end _____

7. welcome any time _____

8. they try to imitate us _____

9. the fake perfumes _____

10. cannot be compared _____

Now decide what is true and what is false.

1. Nearly all Ahmed's family work in the perfume business. (T/F)

2. Brenda has had a look around the store to check out some prices. (T/F)

3. Ahmed lives with his grandfather above the store. (T/F)

4. The perfume business appears to have well guarded trade secrets. (T/F)

5. Ahmed does not admit that his products are a little expensive. (T/F)

6. Ahmed believes his original perfumes are beyond comparison. (T/F)

I'm just looking: three . . . أَنا أَنظُر فَقَط: ثَلاثة

belt	حِزام/أَحزِمة
sleeve	كُمّ/أَكمام
button	زِرّ/أَزرار
collar	ياقَة/ياقات
nightgown	قَميص النَّوم/قُمصان النَّوم
luxurious	فاخِر
souvenir	تَذكار/تَذكارات
crystal	بِلّور/بِلّورات
mother-of-pearl	صَدَف/أَصداف
gold plate	قِشرة الذَّهَب
oak	بَلّوط
beech	زان
ebony	أَبَنوس
sponge	اِسفَنج
tin	صَفيح
precious stone	حَجَر كَريم/أَحجار كَريمة
emerald	زُمُرُّد
turquoise	فَيروز

Local flavor

sequins	تِرتِر
belly-dancing outfit	بَدلة رَقص شَرقي
tailor	خَيّاط/خَيّاطون
cape	جُبّة/جِباب
caftan	قُفطان/قَفاطين
sack, larger (made of jute)	جُوال/جُوالات
sack, smaller (made of denim)	رَكِيبة/رَكائِب
box (made of palm fonds)	قَفَص/أَقفاص
papyrus	وَرق البَرديّ
pharaonic	فِرعَونيّ

Handy extras

I don't care about appearances.	أَنا لا أَهتَمّ بالمَظاهِر.

EXERCISE 8·13

Try to arrange each of the following sets in a logical order of price. Start with what is probably the most expensive, and end with the least.

١ كيلو موز/ساعة ذهب/زِرّ قميص رجاليّ

٢ قَفَص مانجو/بصلة/زُمُرُّدة

٣ سجادة صوف شغل يدويّ/دجاجة مشويّة/جُوال قديم مُستَعمَل وفارغ

٤ كوب ماء بدون ثلج/قميص رجاليّ مفَصّل من الحرير الطبيعيّ/فنجان قهوة بالحليب والسكّر

٥ نصف عود كَرَفس/تذكرة طائرة في الدرجة الأولى حول العالم/بدلة رقص شرقيّ

٦ بعض الزَّيتون/بعض الحَطَب/بعض الأحجار الكريمة

Brenda continues her program about the local traders and craftsmen for her US television channel. Brenda and her interpreter are now interviewing Farouk, who owns a tourist souvenir store.

Brenda: "Tell us, Mr. Farouk, how did you get into the souvenir business?"

فاروق: "أَنا كنتُ بَحّاراً على سفينة لمُدّة عِشرين سنة. جَهَّزتُ مَبلغاً كبيراً من عَمَلي في البحر وإشتَرَيتُ هذا المحلّ من المَرحوم حَمي وأعمل فيه الآن مع نادية، زوجتي."

Brenda: "And what are the most popular items?"

فاروق: "أوّلاً، القُطن المِصريّ لأنّه مَطلوب دائماً. والبَضائع الفَرعونيّة مَرغوبة أيضاً مثل وَرق البَرديّ، والجِمال الصغيرة المَصنوعة من الجلد والمَحشوّة الإِسفِنج."

Brenda: "Do you find that different types of tourists prefer different types of souvenirs?"

فاروق: "نعم. هناك مَن يريدون بدَل الرَّقص الشَّرقيّ مثلاً أو مَن يَطلبون القُفطان التقليديّ أو العَباءات المحليّة. ولكن في النِّهاية، أنا أرى أن الناس تَتَشابَه في ذوقها."

Brenda: "Do you and your wife make all these things yourselves?"

فاروق: "لا. عندنا خَيّاطون لهذه البَضائع وهم يَعمَلون طَوال الأسبوع ما عَدا يوم الجمعة."

Brenda: "So business must be quite good."

فاروق: "نعم. نَشكُر الله."

Brenda: "So, Mr. Farouk, what was the most expensive item you ever sold?"

فاروق: "في يوم جائَتني فتاة جميلة من روسيا وطَلَبَت بَدلة رَقص شَرقيّ تَفصيل من الحرير الطبيعيّ الفاخِر. وبَدَلاً من التِرتر العاديّ أرادَت أن تكون بَدلَتها مُزَيَّنة بالأصداف النادِرة المُستَورَدة وبالأحجار الكَريمة، وطَلَبَت إضافة بعض التَفاصيل من قِشرة ذَهَبيّة، وزُمُرُّدة في وسط مِنطَقة البَطن."

Brenda: "Goodness! How much did she pay for all of this?"

فاروق: "لاشَيء. زوجها دَفَع المَبلَغ كلّه نَقداً وهو يَبتَسِم ولم يُحاوِل أن يُساوِم."

EXERCISE
8·14

Here are some sentences and expressions loosely based on the passage above. Select the English that best represents the Arabic.

١ أنا كنتُ بحّاراً.

I work as a sailor.

I used to be a sailor.

I sat down by the sea.

٢ في يوم جائَتني فتاة جميلة من روسيا.

One day, a beautiful Russian girl came to me.

It takes about a day to prepare this beautiful box.

One day we will sell beautiful Russian souvenirs.

٣ اشتريتُ هذا المحلّ من المَرحوم حَمي.

We had tea with the wholesalers first.

I bought this shop from a wholesaler.

I bought this shop from my late father-in-law.

٤ بدلًا من الترتِر العاديّ

instead of the regular spangles

dancing outfits made of spangles

spangles rather than the other stuff

٥ القُطن المصريّ مطلوب دائماً.

Egyptian cotton is always in demand.

They wanted some Egyptian cotton.

The Egyptian camels are demanding.

٦ الجِمال الصغيرة مصنوعة من الجِلد.

These small camels are Egyptian.

The small camels are made of leather.

My small beautiful things are leather.

٧ الحرير الطبيعيّ الفاخر

luxury, natural silk

luxury mix of silk and leather

luxury, natural leather

٨ إضافة بعض التفاصيل

detailing her demands

adding some details

my demands were added up

٩ دَفَعَ المبلغ كلّه نقداً.

They paid the entire amount in advance.

We cashed-in the entire amount.

He paid the entire amount in cash.

١٠ اِبتَسَمَ ولم يُساوِم.

He haggled but didn't buy.

She didn't smile or haggle.

He smiled and didn't haggle.

Now answer these questions.

1. What is Farouk's wife called?

2. What did Farouk do for a living before he bought the store?

3. How are the little souvenir camels made?

4. How many days a week do the tailors work?

5. What is the most popular item in the store?

6. What material did the girl ask for?

Identify the Arabic expressions that best represent the following and then write them down in the space provided.

1. instead of regular spangles _____

2. (he) paid the whole amount _____

3. We thank God _____

4. rare imported mother of pearl _____

5. I prepared a large sum of money _____

6. A beautiful girl from Russia _____

Law, crime, and justice
الجُزء التاسِع: القانون والجَريمة والعَدالة

Case 1... ١ القَضِية

justice	العَدالة
law	قانون/قَوانين
legal	قانونيّ
investigation	تَحقيق/تَحقيقات
court (house)	مَحكَمة/مَحاكِم
trial	مُحاكَمة/مُحاكَمات
judge	قاضٍ/قُضاة
lawyer	محامٍ/مُحامون
jury member (pl. = jury)	مُحَلَّف/مُحَلَّفون
prosecution	الإدعاء
defense	الدِّفاع
accusation, charge	تُهمة/تُهَم
accused	مُتَّهَم/مُتَّهَمون
gang	عِصابة/عِصابات
victim	ضَحيّة/ضَحايا
crime	جَريمة/جَرائِم
evidence	دَليل/أَدِلّة
fingerprint	بَصمة/بَصمات
weapon	سِلاح/أَسلِحة
ambush	كَمين/كَمائِن
fine	غَرامة/غَرامات
sentence, verdict	حُكم/أَحكام
life sentence	مُؤَبَّد
prison	سِجن/سُجون
prisoner	سَجين/سُجَناء

wing (of prison)	عَنبَر/عَنابِر
prison warden	مَأمور السِّجن
cell	زِنزانة/زِنزانات
misdemeanor	جُنحة/جُنَح
guilty	مُذنِب/مُذنِبون
innocent	بَريء/أَبرِياء
injustice	ظُلم
bribe	رِشوَة/رِشا
appeal	اِستِئناف
clemency	رَأفة
acquittal	بَراءة
amnesty	عَفو

Handy extras

traffic accident	حادِث مُرور/حَوادِث مُرور
criminal law	قانون جِنائيّ/قَوانين جِنائيّة
organized crime	الجَريمة المُنَظَّمة
unknown person	مَجهول/مَجهولون
rule of law	سِيادة القانون
without a license	بِدون رُخصة
good behavior	حُسن السَّير والسُّلوك

EXERCISE
9·1

You are a famous lawyer evaluating some cases then making your pronouncements. Choose the logical ending.

١ في البِداية، كلّ مُتَّهَم _____ (مُخَلَّف/عِصابة/بَريء)

٢ أنتَ ستَدفَع غَرامة بسيطة لأنّه _____ (عَنبَر صغير/حادِث مُرور بسيط/جَريمة كبيرة)

٣ هذه قَضِية ضعيفة لأنّه _____ (لا يوجد دَليل/العِصابة كبيرة/مَأمور السِّجن)

٤ سيَقولون أنّك أنتَ المُذنِب لأنّهم وَجَدوا _____ (عَنبَرك نظيف/بَصماتك على السّلاح/المُؤَيَّد)

٥ حُسن السَّير والسُّلوك سيُساعِدك على _____ (الجَريمة المُنَظَّمة/حَوادِث المُرور/الخُروج من السجن)

٦ لا يوجد مُتَّهَم في هذه القَضِية. المُتَّهَم _____ (غير مُناسِب/مَجهول/جُنحة)

It's action time

to pursue (chase)	طارَد/يُطارِد
to arrest	قَبَض (على)/يَقبِض (على)
to confess	إعتَرَف/يعتَرِف
to warn	أنذَر/يُنذِر
to discipline	أدَّب/يُؤَدِّب
to imprison	سَجَن/يَسجُن
to accuse	اتَّهَم/يَتَّهِم
to order	أمَر/يَأمُر
to defend	دافَع/يُدافِع
to reward	كافَأ/يُكافِئ
to forge	زَوَّر/يُزَوِّر
to murder	قَتَل/يَقتُل
to embezzle	اختَلَس/يَختَلِس
to steal	سَرَق/يَسرِق
to rape	اغتَصَب/يَغتَصِب
to kidnap	خَطَف/يَخطِف
to stab	طَعَن/يَطعَن
to strangle	خَنَق/يَخنُق
to provoke	استَفَزّ/يَستَفِزّ
to smuggle	هَرَّب/يُهَرِّب
to escape	هَرَب/يَهرُب

Note how the words for "to smuggle" and "to escape" are differentiated only by how they are vowelized. Given that most Arabic is written without vowel signs, the reader has to rely almost entirely on the context to decide what is meant.

Local flavors

gallows	مَشنَقة/مَشانِق
swordsman	سَيّاف/سَيّافون

Here are some 'hard luck' stories as told by criminals. Complete the English version of their stories to match the Arabic.

١ بعد أن قَتَلتُها قَبَضوا عليَّ في كَمين. ظُلم!

After I _____ her they _____ me in an _____. Injustice!

٢ أنا خَنَقتُهُ أوّلاً، وبعد ذلك خَطَفتُهُ.

I _____ him first, and then I _____ him.

٣ اِستَفَزَّني فطَعَنتُهُ.

He _____ me so I _____ him.

٤ هي ليسَت مُختَلِسة حقيقيّة. كانَت سَتُعيد كلّ شيء.

She is not a real _____. She was going to give _____ back.

٥ أنا الآن عندي سِلاح ورُخصة، فسَأقتُلُهُ يوم الثُّلاثاء.

Now I have a _____ and a _____, so I'll kill him on _____.

٦ هل هناك رَأفة لثلاث جَرائِم قَتل وجَريمة اِغتِصاب واحدة؟

Is there any _____ for three _____ of murder and one crime of _____?

Karim and Samir have just met. Read the dialogue between them.

كريم: "أهلاً وسهلاً. أنا اسمي كريم. أنا بريء."

سمير: "أهلاً بك يا سيّد كريم. وأنا اسمي سمير. أنا أيضاً بريء."

كريم: "أهلاً وسهلاً بالسيّد سمير. ولكن لو كُنتَ بريئاً، ماذا تَفعَل في هذه الزِّنزانة؟"

سمير: "في الحقيقة يا أخي كريم أنا ضَحيّة. جارَتي كانَت سيّدة غنيّة جدّاً وأنا فقير. أمَرتُها أن تُعطيني بعض المال أو الذَّهَب أو الأحجار الكريمة لأنّني كُنتُ أريد أن أشتري بعض السَّتائر الجديدة لحُجرة الجُلوس، ولكنّها قالَت "لا!". فشَعَرتُ أنّني ضَحيّة وخَنَقتُها أوّلاً ثمّ طَعَنتُها بخَنجَري المَسموم وأخَذتُ المَبلَغ الذي أحتاجُهُ للسَّتائر."

كريم: "أكيد بريء. أكيد ضَحيّة. لو كانَت هناك عَدالة في هذه المدينة ستَدفَع غَرامة بسيطة وتَخرُج من السِّجن اليوم أو غداً."

سمير: "هذا لو كانَت هناك عدالة! ولكن أين العدالة؟ أين العدالة اليوم يا سيد كريم؟ وأنت يا سيدي؟ ماذا تفعل هنا؟"

كريم: "في الحقيقة يا أخي سمير أنا أيضاً ضَحيّة. كان حادِث مُرور بسيط. أنا أعمل في بنك وكُنتُ أريد أن أشتري إطارات جديدة لسيّارتي. أخَذتُ من البنك بعض زكائِب الذَّهَب وجُوالات المال وصَناديق الأحجار الكريمة ووضعتُها في سيّارتي واتَّجَهتُ إلى بَوّابة خُروج السيّارات. وَقَفَ مدير البنك أمام سيّارتي وقال "لا!" فخَنَقتُهُ ثمّ طَعَنتُهُ بخَنجَري المَسموم. ماذا أفعل؟ كان يَقِف في طريق السيّارة. لم أتَمَكَّن من المُرور!"

سمير: "نعم، حادِث مُرور بسيط. أكيد بريء. أكيد ضَحيّة. أين العَدالة يا ناس؟!"

Select the English phrase that best represents the Arabic.

١ لو كُنتَ بريءٌ

if you are innocent

when they see you are guilty

she knew I was innocent

٢ أنا ضحيّة

she is innocent

I am a victim

I am not guilty

٣ جارتي سيّدة غنيّة

he is not innocent

my neighbor is a rich lady

my wife heard them sing

٤ لو كانت هناك عدالة

if there were justice

we are counting on you

the judge is over there

٥ ستخرج من السجن اليوم أو غداً

they will see you are innocent

you'll be out of jail today or tomorrow

he will spend a few days in jail

٦ إطارات جديدة لسيّارتي

new cars for the boys

new tires for my car

new boys in the car park

٧ خَنَقتُهُ ثمّ طَعَنتُها

I strangled him then I stabbed her

she stabbed me through the heart

I heard him strangle her

٨ بوّابة الخروج

the exit gate

the guards by the exit

the entrance is there

٩ لم أتمكّن من المرور

I couldn't see the lights

I saw the traffic jam

I couldn't go through

١٠ كان يقف في طريقي

he was standing in my way

he was sitting in his car

she was standing by her car

EXERCISE
9·4

Select the Arabic sentence that best represents the English.

١ What are you doing here?

هل هي هنا أم هناك؟

ماذا تفعل هنا؟

متى وصلتَ هنا؟

٢ She was a very rich lady.

سيّارتي سريعة وغالية.

كانت سيّدة غنيّة جدّاً.

كانت سيّدة سريعة وجميلة.

٣ We have old curtains in the living room.

في الحجرة ستائر جديدة وستائر قديمة.

عندنا ستائر قديمة في حجرة الجلوس.

عندهم مجلس جديد وراء الستائر القديمة.

She wants new tires for her car. ٤

عندها سيّارة جديدة وإطارات قديمة.

هي تريد إطارات جديدة لسيّارتها.

تريد أن تُجَرِّب هذه السيّارة الجديدة.

He stabbed me with his poisoned dagger. ٥

طَعَنَني بِخَنجَره المسموم.

سأَطعَنُهُ يوم السبت بعد الظهر.

سأَطعَن الشخص الذي طَعَنَني.

I took the amount I needed. ٦

أعطيتُهُ المبلغ الذي طلبه.

أخذتُ المبلغ الذي أحتاجه.

أنت لا تحتاج إلى كلّ هذا المبلغ.

Where is the justice, people?! ٧

أين العَدالة يا ناس؟!

أين الجريمة يا ناس؟!

أين الظُّلم يا عزيزي؟!

EXERCISE
9·5

Now answer these questions about Karim and Samir.

1. Where did they meet?

2. What did Samir need to buy?

3. Whom did Samir ask for money?

4. Where does Karim work?

5. Who stood in front of Karim's car?

6. What was the extra ingredient added to their daggers?

Decide what is true and what is false.

1. Karim and Samir are innocent victims. (T/F)

2. Samir and Karim are partners in a law firm. (T/F)

3. Karim helped himself to sack-loads of cash and gold. (T/F)

4. Samir strangled his neighbor. (T/F)

5. Karim and Samir will probably pay small fines. (T/F)

6. Karim was driving towards the exit when he saw the manager. (T/F)

7. Karim and Samir use a similar technique in dealing with rejection. (T/F)

Handy extras

This is legally sound.	هذا سَليم من الناحِية القانونيّة.
These measures are illegal.	هذه الإجراءات غير قانونيّة.

Case 2... ٢ ...القَضِية

assault	اِعتِداء/اِعتِداءات
armed robbery	سَطو مُسَلَّح
serial killer	سَفّاح/سَفّاحون
ransom	فِدية
masked man (face and head wrapped with scarf)	رَجُل مُلَثَّم/رِجال مُلَثَّمون
fabricated case	قَضِيّة مُلَفَّقة/قَضايا مُلَفَّقة
witness	شاهِد/شُهود
verbal agreement	اِتِّفاق شَفوي/اِتِّفاقات شَفويّة
oath	قَسَم
confiscation	مُصادَرة
banned	مَمنوع
final warning	تَحذير نِهائِيّ

Our local paper is being accused of sensationalism. Read some of their recent headlines, then choose the Arabic that best conveys the meaning as closely as possible.

ORGANIZED CRIME REWARDED! ١

Our town, now global capital of money laundering.

مَطلوب مَبلَغ كبير!

مُنَظَّمة خَيريّة ستدفع مُكافأة للعُمّال.

مُكافأة للجريمة المُنَظَّمة!

مدينَتنا الآن عاصِمة غَسيل الأموال في العالَم.

كلّ الغَسيل في غَسّالة المَلابِس!

مدينَتنا النظيفة هي عاصِمة الغَسّالات في العالَم.

IS JUSTICE CLOSED ON FRIDAYS? ٢

Friday morning armed robbery in restaurant.

هل العَدالة مُغلَقة يوم الجمعة؟

سَطو مُسَلَّح في مطعم صباح يوم الجمعة.

هل هذا المطعم مُغلَق يوم الجمعة؟

سَطو مُسَلَّح بجوار المَدخَل الرئيسيّ كلّ يوم خميس.

هل سَتعَود العَدالة يوم الجمعة؟

الجَريمة المُنَظَّمة لا تَعمَل يوم الجمعة.

RAPE OF OUR TOWN CONTINUES! ٣

Armed gangs have now bought our streets.

من سيَشتَري هذا الشارع!

شَوارِعنا الآن للبيع أو للإيجار لأعلى سِعر.

إغتِصاب مدينَتنا كلّ يوم!

الجريمة المُنَظَّمة والعِصابات المُسَلَّحة في كلّ شارع.

إغتِصاب مدينتنا يَستَمرّ!

العِصابات المُسَلَّحة اِشتَرَت شَوارِعنا الآن.

COURT OR CIRCUS? ٤

Witnesses assaulted by masked man.

سيرك في المَحكَمة؟

المُحامون والقُضاة هم رِجال القانون الجِنائيّ.

مَحكَمة ولكنّها سيرك؟

الشُّهود المُلَثَّمون يَشهَدون في المَحكَمة.

مَحكَمة أم سيرك؟

رجل مُلَثَّم يَعتَدي على الشُّهود.

VICTIM OF CRIME ARRESTED! ٥

Owner of three-tire car fined.

الجريمة المُنَظَّمة تَستَمِرّ!

سنَحتاج إلى اِستِمارة وثلاث صُوَر حَديثة.

القَبض على ضَحيّة الجريمة!

غَرامة لِصاحِب سيّارة بثلاثة إطارات.

إطارات السيّارات لِلبيع!

ثلاثة إطارات لِلبيع بسِعر مُغرٍ اليوم فقط.

EMBEZZLER TO GO! ٦

Pizza man innocent of stealing dough.

المُختَلِس سيَخرُج!

رجل البيتزا بريء من سَرِقة العَجين.

سنَذهَب إلى المُختَلِس!

بيتزا لكلّ الناس في بيتي يوم الخميس القادم.

المُختَلِسون سيَأكُلونها!

اِختِلاس بيتزا كبيرة بالجُبن والطماطم.

The editor of our local paper categorically denies being sensationalist. Read the statement he issued to the press.

نحن نَعيش هنا في مدينَتنا التي كانَت جميلة. ولكن الآن نحن لا نَعرِف: هل العَدالة في إجازة؟ هل القانون نائِم؟ أين ضُبّاط الأمن؟ العِصابات المُسَلَّحة في الشَّوارِع في الليل وفي النهار. السيّارات تَختَفي من الضَّواحي التي كانت مَطلوبة. الأثاث يَختَفي من البُيوت التي كانت مَرغوبة. إنّهم يَسرِقون حقائِب السُّوّاح من على رَصيف المِيناء. نعم! ويَسرِقون مَقاعِد الرُّكّاب من على رصيف الانتِظار في محطّة القطار. هذه قَطَرات في المُحيط! مُحيط من الجريمة المُنَظَّمة. وضُبّاط الأمن يُضَيِّعون وَقتَهُم ووقتنا باستِمرار.

أنا وأُسرتي لا نَخرُج من بيتنا بعد غُروب الشمس. نحن نَعيش في دائِرة من الخَوف، والجَريدة هي صَوت هذا الخَوف. هذه الجَريدة هي صَوت الحَقيقة.

EXERCISE
9·8

Find the Arabic expression that best represents the following phrases taken from the editor's statement. Then write the Arabic below the English.

1. We live in a circle of fear.

_____

2. Is justice on vacation?

_____

3. Where are the security officers?

_____

4. neighborhoods that used to be in demand

_____

5. They are stealing the tourists' bags.

_____

6. houses that used to be desirable

_____

7. We don't go out after sunset.

_____

8. This paper is the voice of truth.

_____

Now answer the questions about the editor's statement.

1. How have in-demand neighborhoods changed?

2. Who roams the streets all night and all day?

3. What disappears from desirable homes?

4. What goes missing from the port quay?

5. When does the editor's family stop going out?

6. What gets stolen from the train station?

Choose the most logical ending from the three options.

١ قَبَضوا على ابني لأن سيّارته _____ (بِلا رُخصة/لَونها أصفر/للبيع)

٢ جَلَسَ الناس في المَحكَمة وانتَظَروا دُخول _____ (المُستَشفى/القاضي/فَصل الشِّتاء)

٣ قالَت أمّي للقاضي إنّني بَريء وأن كلّ هذه التُّهَم _____ (للإيجار/مُلَفَّقة/لَونها لَيمونيّ)

٤ ضُبّاط الأمن طارَدوا العِصابة _____ (ثلاثة أكواب/لِيَدهُنوا الجُدران/في الشَّوارع)

٥ وَجَدناه بسُرعة لأنّه تَرَكَ بَصمات أصابِعه على _____ (البرازيل/الخِنجَر/حَساء الخُضرَوات والدَّجاج)

٦ لو ساعَدتَنا واعتَرَفتَ بتفاصيل الجريمة سنَطلُب من القاضي أن _____ (يُعامِلك بالرَّأفة/يَلعَب تنس/يَشرَب كولا)

Case 3 ... ٣ القَضيّة

enemy of the people	عَدوّ الشَّعب/أعداء الشَّعب
state security	أمن الدَّولة
political activist	ناشِط سِياسيّ/نُشَطاء سِياسيّون
authority	سُلطة/سُلطات
resistance	مُقاوَمة
dissident	مُنشَقّ/مُنشَقّون
troublemaker	مُشاغِب/مُشاغِبون
blogger	مُدَوِّن/مُدَوِّنون
analyst	مُحَلِّل/مُحَلِّلون

commentator	مُعَلِّق / مُعَلِّقون
espionage	تَجَسُّس
terrorism	إرهاب
sabotage	تَخريب
bomb	قُنبُلة / قَنابِل
extremism	تَطَرُّف
censorship	رِقابة
corruption	فَساد
apology	اِعتِذار / اِعتِذارات
immunity	حَصانة / حَصانات
reaction	رَدّ فِعل / رُدود أَفعال
political regime	نِظام سِياسيّ / أَنظِمة سِياسيّة
nuclear energy	الطّاقة الذَّرِّيّة
solar energy	الطّاقة الشَّمسيّة
republic	جُمهوريّة / جُمهوريّات
republican	جُمهوريّ / جُمهوريّون
kingdom	مَملَكة / مَمالِك
royalist	مَلَكيّ
royal family	العائِلة المَلَكيّة / العائِلات المَلَكيّة
heir apparent	وَلي العَهد

EXERCISE 9·11

Choose the most logical ending from the three options.

١ هذا الولد يُسَبِّب لنا المَشاكِل لأنّه _____ (المَلِك / ليس حَقيقيّ / مُشاغِب)

٢ أوّل وأكبر أبناء المَلِك هو _____ (المُنشَقّ / الطّاقة الشَّمسيّة / وَلي العَهد)

٣ قالوا أنّه عَدو الشَّعب لأنّه _____ (وَقَف ضِدّ الفَساد / يحِبّ الجُبن والطماطم / اسمه أحمد)

٤ نحن نعيش في مَملَكة ونِظامنا السِّياسيّ _____ (لا يخرُج بعد الغُروب / مَلَكيّ / بثلاثة إطارات)

٥ الطّاقة الذَّرِّيّة من الذَّرة، ولكن الطّاقة الشَّمسيّة من _____ (العائِلة / الشَّمس / القانون)

٦ يَجِب علينا أن نَقِف معاً في مُقاوَمة _____ (الإرهاب والتَّطَرُّف / أُمَّهاتنا وأبائنا / فَصل الرَّبيع)

Karim and Samir have gone to separate jails where they will probably be spending the rest of their lives. Read Karim's postcard to his mother.

عزيزتي ماما،

أنا الآن عندي أصدِقاء كثيرون في السِجن. صديقي مُحسِن يقول أنّه ناشِط سِياسيّ ومُشاغِب وهو يريد نِظاماً جُمهوريّاً لأنّه لا يحبّ المَلِك، ولكن أنا لا أعرِف لِماذا، أنا أرى أن المَلِك لطيف وعنده مَلابِس مُلَوَّنة. صديقي إبراهيم يقول أنه يريد الطاقة الشَّمسيّة فقط لأنّها نظيفة، وحاوَلَ تَخريب شيء ما في مَبنى الطاقة الذَرّيّة ولكن في الحقيقة أنا لا أعرِف الفَرق. وشَوقي مَشهور بأنّه يَكرَه السُّلطات ويُقاوِمها طوال الوقت وأنّه العَدو رَقم واحد للضُّبّاط في أمن الدَّولة. وعندي صديق جديد اسمه أنوَر ولكن كلّ الناس تُسَمّيه "الدكتور" لأنّه مُدَوِّن ومُحَلِّل ومُعَلِّق سِياسيّ ويُثَرثِر كثيراً. في البِداية أنا كُنتُ أظُنّ أن "مُحَلِّل ومُعَلِّق" مَعناها "حَلّاق" ولكن بلُغة عربيّة عالية جدّاً. يوجد مَعنا في العَنبَر أخصائيّ تَجَسُّس وإرهاب وتَخريب من دَولة أُخرى ولكن أنا لا أفهَم ما يقول. لا يوجد أيّ شَخص بريء هنا غيري.

ابنك،

كريم

(ماما، ربما من الأفضل أن تبيعي سيارتي.)

EXERCISE
9·12

Decide which of the following about Karim's letter is true and which is false.

1. Mohsin is a republican and a troublemaker. (T/F)

2. Karim tried to blow up the atomic energy building. (T/F)

3. The guy they call 'the doctor' is also a barber. (T/F)

4. Karim knows the difference between nuclear and solar energy. (T/F)

5. Anwar talks a lot. (T/F)

6. Karim enjoys chatting with the foreign sabotage specialist. (T/F)

EXERCISE
9·13

Now, answer these questions about the postcard.

1. What does Shawky hate?

2. Why does Ibrahim want solar energy only?

3. Who is the number one enemy of the state security officers?

4. Why does Mohsin want a republican regime?

5. What did Karim think "analyst and commentator" meant?

6. Why does Karim approve of the king?

Choose the English that best represents the Arabic sentence.

١ في الحقيقة أنا لا أعرِف الفَرق.

In truth, the difference is very small.

In truth, I don't really care about it.

In truth, I don't know the difference.

٢ إنّه يقول أنّه ناشِط سِياسيّ.

She brushes her hair in the afternoon.

He likes to take a nap after lunch.

He says he is a political activist.

٣ أنتَ عَدو الضُّباط في أمن الدَّولة.

You are the enemy of state security officers.

He is an enemy of the people, say the officers.

We need some enemies to create more officers.

٤ أصدِقائي المُشاغِبون لا يُحبّون الملك.

The king secretly likes troublemakers a lot.

My troublemaker friends don't like the king.

The friendly king loves other kings and queens.

٥ حاوَلَ تَخريب شيء ما.

He tried to sabotage something.

They almost destroyed his chances.

She sabotaged it and they know it.

٦ إنّها أخصائيّة تَجَسُّس وإرهاب وتَخريب.

She is a beautician who specializes in slimming and massage.

She is a specialist in espionage, terrorism and sabotage.

She pretends to know everything about espionage and slimming.

Freedom الحُرّيّة/الحُرّيّات

freedom of the press	حُرّيّة الصَّحافة
freedom of thought	حُرّيّة الفِكر
freedom of belief	حُرّيّة الاِعتِقاد
freedom of movement	حُرّيّة الحَركة
freedom of assembly	حُرّيّة التَّجَمُّع
freedom of speech	حُرّيّة التَّحَدُّث
freedom of worship	حُرّيّة العبادة
freedom of expression	حُرّيّة التَّعبير

Circumstances

circumstances can change	من المُمكِن أن تَتَغَيَّر الظُّروف
in mysterious circumstances	في ظُروف غَامِضَة
under normal circumstances	في الظُّروف العَاديّة
in the current circumstances	في الظُّروف الحاليّة
these are exceptional circumstances	هذه ظُروف اِستِثنائيّة
emergency circumstances	ظُروف طارِئة
depending on circumstances	على حَسب الظُّروف
unfavorable circumstances	ظُروف غَير مُواتيّة

News flash: we are getting unconfirmed reports that in Samir's prison a mutiny is raging. The warden has asked his senior officers for a written report. More soon . . .

It's action time

to reform	أَصلَح/يُصلِح
to condemn	شَجَب/يَشجُب
to monitor	راقَب/يُراقِب
to occupy	اِحتَلّ/يَحتَلّ
to respect	اِحتَرَم/يَحتَرِم
to sacrifice	ضَحَّى/يُضَحّي
to negotiate	فاوَض/يُفاوِض
to escalate	صَعَّد/يُصَعِّد

Events, dear boy. Events. الأَحداث يا وَلَدي العَزيز. الأَحداث.

revolution	ثَورة/ثَورات
demonstrations	مُظاهَرات
obscenities	بَذاءات
anarchy	فَوضى
occupation	اِحتِلال
aggression	عُدوان
tolerance	تَسامُح
intolerance	تَشَدُّد
statistic	إِحصائِيّة/إِحصائِيّات
army	جَيش/جُيوش
military; soldier	عَسكَرِيّ/عَسكَرِيّون
civilian	مَدَنِيّ/مَدَنِيّون
popular; people's	شَعبِيّ
elections	اِنتِخابات
candidate	مُرَشَّح/مُرَشَّحون
influence	نُفوذ

Handy extras

times of hardship	وَقت الشِّدّة/أوقات الشِّدّة
time bomb	قُنبُلة زَمَنِيّة/قَنابِل زَمَنِيّة
unsavory remarks	تَعليقات غير مُستَساغة
official spokesperson	مُتَحَدِّث رَسمِيّ/مُتَحَدِّثون رَسمِيّون
complete silence	صَمت تامّ
Do these rebels have specific demands?	هل لِهؤُلاء المُتَمَرِّدين مَطالِب مُحَدَّدة ؟
Their leader is wanted alive or dead.	قائِدُهُم مَطلوب حَيّاً أو مَيِّتاً.
I will never abdicate the throne.	أنا لَن أتَنازَل عَن العَرش أبَداً.

Read these leaked extracts from the report prepared for the warden by his senior officers in Samir's prison.

تَقرير رَسمِيّ إلى السَيِّد مَأمور السِّجن:

بَدَأَت المُظاهَرات بعد صَلاة الفَجر مُباشَرةً في العَنبَر الغَربِيّ رَقم ثلاثة وهو عَنبَر المُشاغِبين. خَرَجَ المُتَمَرِّدون من الزِّنزانات وساروا في اِتِّجاه المَطعَم لاِحتِلاله وتَخريبه. نحن سَمِعنا البَذاءات ورَأَينا الفَوضى من شِبّاك غرفة الضُّبّاط فَنَزَلنا بِسُرعة لِنُفاوِضهُم.

يَبدو أن قائِدهُم والمتَحَدِّث الرَّسميّ هو السَّجين رقم ٨٩٩ه٤٥ فسَأَلناه إن كانَت لَهُم مَطالِب مُحَدَّدة فقال: "أنا أُدافِع عن حُقوقِنا فقط. هناك فَساد ورِشوة في المطعم. السُّجَناء السِّياسيّون في العَنبَر الشَّرقيّ رقم تِسعة يأكُلون الفاكِهة كلّ يوم تقريباً ونحن لا نأكُل الفاكِهة إلا يوم الجمعة فقط، وهذه لَيسَت عَدالة."

قُلنا لَهُم أنّنا نَشجُب أيّ فَساد أو رِشوة داخل هذه الجُدران، ولكن التَّظاهر مَمنوع في قوانين السِّجن. وبعد أن تَفاوَضنا معهم وَصَلنا إلى اتِّفاق شَفويّ وهو أن يَتَوَقَّفوا عن التَّصعيد وأن يَعودوا إلى الزِنزانات ونحن سنَطلُب من المَأمور التَّحقيق، وستَكون هناك إصلاحات فَوراً.

EXERCISE 9·15

Match the opposites.

يعود إلى الزِّنزانة	١ العَنبَر الغَربيّ
ظُروف اِستِثنائيّة	٢ بعد الصَّلاة
مُتَساهِل	٣ اِتِّفاق شَفويّ
قبل الصَّلاة	٤ مُتَشَدِّد
اتِّفاق مَكتوب	٥ يخرُج من الزِّنزانة
العَنبَر الشَّرقيّ	٦ ظُروف عَاديّة

EXERCISE 9·16

Select the English sentence that best represents the Arabic.

١ المُظاهَرات والتَمَرُّد داخِل السِّجن هي ظُروف اِستِثنائيّة.

It appears there is a mutiny inside the prison but we cannot be sure.

Demonstrations and mutiny inside the prison are exceptional circumstances.

We have heard unconfirmed reports that some of the prison guards are involved.

٢ كَتَبنا هذا التَّقرير الرَّسميّ وسنُقَدِّمه إلى المَأمور.

We will not negotiate with the warden after what happened today.

The warden has asked to see us in his office first thing Monday.

We have written this official report and will present it to the warden.

٣ ضُبّاط الأمن يشجُبون أي فَساد أو رِشوة داخِل جُدران السجن.

The security officers condemn any violence inside the prison cells.

The security officers will not tolerate any disturbances in the restaurant area.

The security officers condemn any corruption or bribery within the prison walls.

٤ ستَجِد السُّجَناء السِّياسيِّين في العَنبَر الشَّرقيِّ.

You will find the political prisoners in the Eastern wing.

The warden and the demonstrators are in the Eastern wing.

The Western wing usually houses all the troublemakers.

٥ وَصَلنا في النِّهاية إلى اتِّفاق شَفويٍّ.

We arrived at the end, and it was all over.

In the end, we reached a verbal agreement.

We agree that the ending could have been different.

٦ يبدو لي أن المُتَمَرِّدين لَهُم مَطالِب مُحَدَّدة

It seems the rebels don't know what they really want.

I believe the rebels will accept whatever we offer them.

It seems to me that the rebels have specific demands.

EXERCISE
9·17

Circle the reasonable ending, then write it in the space provided.

١ قال قائِدُهُم: "أنا أُدافِع عن _____" (الفَساد / حُقوقنا / المَأمور)

٢ يبدو أن قائِدهُم له _____ (نُفوذ / ظُروف غَامِضة / وَلي عَهد)

٣ بَدَأَت المُظاهَرات بعد _____ (يوم الجمعة / صَلاة الفَجر / وُصول الملك)

٤ تَوَقَّفوا عن التَّصعيد الآن وعادوا إلى _____ (المطعم / الزِّنزانات / الفَوضى)

٥ هل يوجد بينكم قائد يَستَطيع أن _____؟ (يُفاوِض المَأمور / يأكُل الفاكِهة / يُراقِب الجُدران)

٦ المَأمور رَجُل مُتَساهِل ولطيف مثل الملك وسنَصِل إلى _____ (بَصمات / اتِّفاق / تَخريب)

Business and politics

الجُزء العاشِر: الأَعْمال و السِّياسَة

On top of the tree فَوق قِمَّة الشَّجَرة

board (of directors)	مَجلِس الإدارة/ مَجالِس الإدارة
chairman of the Board	رَئيس مَجلِس الإدارة
managing director	العُضو المُنتَدَب
partner	شَريك/ شُرَكاء
founder	مُؤَسِّس/ مُؤَسِّسون
manager	مُدير/ مُدَراء
member	عُضو/ أَعضاء
financier	مُمَوِّل/ مُمَوِّلون
intermediary	وَسيط/ وسَطاء
marketing expert	خَبير تَسويق/ خُبَراء تَسويق
specialist	اِختِصاصيّ/ اِختِصاصيّون
consultant	اِستِشاريّ/ اِستِشاريّون
accountant	مُحاسِب/ مُحاسِبون
capable	كُفء/ أَكْفَاء
perfects his work	يُتقِن عَملهُ/ يُتقِنون عَملهُم
does his work	يُؤَدِّي عَملهُ/ يُؤَدّون عَملهُم
researcher	باحِث/ باحِثُون
trader	تاجِر/ تُجّار
committee	لَجنة/ لِجان
shareholders	حَمَلة الأسهُم

Notice that العُضو المُنتَدَب is "the member of the board who has been nominated, selected and assigned" (to run the business day-to-day on behalf of the other members).

Choose the Arabic word that best conveys the general meaning of the English.

مُحاسِب/باحِثُون/تَسويق/رَئيس/وَسيط/مَجلِس/مُؤسِّس

_____ place where people sit ١

_____ person who lays foundation ٢

_____ person dealing with calculation ٣

_____ people who search for things ٤

_____ person who operates in the middle ٥

_____ activities related to the market ٦

_____ head person, at top seat ٧

Handy extras

at my desk by seven	على مَكتَبي في السابِعَة
out and about all day	أَلُفّ وأَدور طَوالَ اليوم
to turn; to spin	لَفَّ/يَلُفّ؛ دارَ/يَدور

يَلُفّ ويَدور: Going around in circles. This is used both for one "beating around the bush" and not getting to the point, or more literally when having difficulty finding an address, for example.

Around the tree حَول الشَّجَرة

capital	رَأس مال/رُؤوس أموال
arrangement	تَرتيب/تَرتيبات
expenses; fees	نَفَقات
salary	مُرتَّب/مُرتَّبات
basic salary	مُرتَّب أَساسي/مُرتَّبات أَساسيّة
deal	صَفقَة/صَفقات
budget	ميزانيّة/ميزانيّات
token contribution	مُشارَكة بَسيطة
brief summary	موجَز مُختَصَر
independence	اِستِقلال
ally	حَليف/حُلَفاء
enemy	عَدوّ/أعداء

friction	اِحتِكاك / اِحتِكاكات
crisis	أزمة / أزَمات
terse statement	بَيان مُقتَضَب / بَيانات مُقتَضَبة
monopoly	اِحتِكار / اِحتِكارات
merger	اِندِماج / اِندِماجات
unemployment	بِطالة
memorandum	مُذَكِّرة / مُذَكِّرات
colleague	زَميل / زُمَلاء
recession	كَساد
creativity	اِبتِكار
art	فَنّ / فُنون
promotional activity	نَشاط تَرويجيّ / أنشِطة تَرويجيّة
public relations	عَلاقات عامّة
branch	فَرع / فُروع
commercial law	قانون تِجاريّ / قَوانين تِجاريّة
limited liability	مَسئوليّة مَحدودة
partnership agreement	اِتِّفاق مُشاركة
nominal value	قيمَة اِسميّة
profit	رِبح / أرباح
shares and bonds	الأسهُم السَّنَدات
corporation	شَرِكة مُساهَمة / شَرِكات مُساهَمة
chamber of commerce	الغُرفَة التِجاريّة
privilege	ميزَة / مَزايا
goods and services	بَضائع وخَدَمات

EXERCISE
10·2

Choose the Arabic phrase that best conveys the main point of the sentence.

١ قال الرئيس في بَيان مُقتَضَب أن الكَساد هو العَدوّ.

بيان الرئيس فيه فنّ.

بيان الرئيس قصير.

بيان الرئيس تجاريّ.

٢ سَنَحتاج إلى مُضاعَفَة الإنتاج والنَشاط التَّرويجيّ.

الإنتاج يَجِب أَن يَتَوَقَّف.

الإنتاج يَجِب أَن يَزيد.

الإنتاج يجب أَن يَلُفَّ ويَدور.

٣ كَتَبَ المدير المذكِّرة وأَرسَلَها اليوم إلى الرئيس.

المذكِّرة مكتوبة للرئيس.

الرئيس سيكتب المذكِّرة.

المجلس سيكتب للمدير.

٤ سَيَقِف محمّد رَمزيّ معي لأنّه حَليفي الوَحيد في مجلس الإدارة.

أعضاء المجلس أعدائي ما عدا محمّد رَمزيّ.

أعضاء المجلس خُلَفائي ومحمّد رَمزيّ عدوّي.

ليس عندي أي أعداء بين أعضاء المجلس.

٥ يُحَلِّل المحاسب الأرقام، مثل النفقات والأرباح وأسعار الأسهم.

المُحامي يَهتَمّ بالأرقام والنفقات.

المحاسب يعرف الأرقام لأنّها مهمّة.

المحاسب لن يُحَلِّل أسعار الأسهم.

٦ شَرِكَتنا كبيرة وتَهتَمّ بالقوانين التِّجارية السَّليمة في كلّ نَشاطها.

نشاطنا قانونيّ وسليم.

محامي الشركة هو المحاسب.

النشاط السليم لا يهتمّ بالقانون.

٧ المُرَتَّبات والمَزايا جُزء من نَفَقات الشركة.

الشركة لا تَدفَع نفقاتها.

المُرَتَّبات تأتينا من شركة أخرى.

الشركة تدفع المُرَتَّبات والمزايا.

٨ هذا المَبلَغ هو مُشاركة بَسيطة من الزُّمَلاء في المكتب.

هذا المبلغ ليس كبيراً جدّاً.

هذا المكتب مَوجود في الشركة.

أنا ومحمّد رمزيّ في مكتب واحد.

Choose the phrase that best completes the sentence.

١ مُرَتَّبي الأساسيّ وحده لا يكفيني لأن ‬ـــــــــــ‬ (بيان الرئيس قصير/نفقاتي كثيرة/زملائي يحللون الأسعار)

٢ حدث احتكاك بين المحاسب وأعضاء المجلس والمدير لأنهم ‬ـــــــــــ‬ (يرتّبون الميزانية/يذاكرون/في الحقيبة)

٣ هذه السنة أفضل من السنة الماضية لأن ‬ـــــــــــ‬ (المذكّرة مكتوبة/الأرباح أعلى/محمد رمزي لا يهتم)

٤ لا داعي للتفاصيل الكثيرة في المذكّرة، يكفيهم ‬ـــــــــــ‬ (مبلغ بسيط/مكتب واحد/مُوجَز مُختَصَر)

٥ لا يُمكِن أن تكون شَرِكَتنا هي الشركة الوَحيدة في السوق لأن هذا ‬ـــــــــــ‬ (مزايا/احتكار/فُروع)

٦ لو اِتَّفَقَت شَرِكَتنا مع شركتهم ستكون هذه هي ‬ـــــــــــ‬ (بَيان مُقتَضَب/الأسهُم والسَندات/صفقة العام)

Handy extras

We would like to know the employees' opinion.	نُريد أن نَعرِف رَأي المُوَظَّفين.
What is the staff's point of view?	ما هي وَجهة نَظَر العامِلين؟
Now, a word from our sponsor.	والآن، كَلِمة من الشَّرِكة الكَفيلة.
Our correspondent in the capital has the full story.	مُراسِلنا في العاصِمة لَدَيه القِصّة الكامِلة.
She was our war correspondent for three years.	كانَت مُراسِلَتنا الحَربيّة لِمُدّة ثَلاث سَنَوات.
Our royal correspondent took this photograph.	مُراسِلنا المَلَكيّ أَخَذَ هذه الصورة.

Fawzi is a successful businessman running a small media empire. Here are highlights of an interview he gave to one of his own magazines.

هل تُريدون القِصّة الكامِلة؟ أنا بَدَأتُ من لاشيء. بائِع مَجَلات وجَرائِد ألُفّ وأدور طَوالَ النَّهار، وطالِب ومُتَرجِم في الليل. واليوم أنا رئيس مَجلِس الإدارة، وأجلس فَوق قِمّة الشَّجرة. ولكن سَتَجِدني على مَكتَبي قبل السابعة كلّ يوم. أنا لا أُحِبّ الإجازات ورحلاتي كلّها رِحلات عَمَل لِزيارة مَكاتِبنا حَولَ العالَم.

في البِداية كان كلّ رَأس ماليّ هنا ... في رأسي وفي قَلبي. أنا دائِماً أَقِف وَحدي أمام العالَم، لا شَريك ولا كَفيل ولا مُمَوِّل. كلّ هذه الشركة هي من عرق جَبيني وَحدي. أنا المؤَسِّس الوَحيد. لا يوجد عندي لِجان تَلُفّ وتَدور حول لاشيء ولا حَمَلة أسهُم يقولون لي "لا!". ومع كلّ هذا، هل تَعرِفون أَنَّني آخُذ مُرَتَّبي فقط مِثل كلّ الزُّمَلاء؟ نعم! كل الأرباح تَعود إلى الشركة.

Choose the logical ending.

١ كان فوزي يلفّ ويدور طوال النهار لأنّه كان ــــــــــــــــــــــ

يعمل في لَجنة.

يريد أن يجلس.

يبيع المجلات.

٢ فوزي يجلس الآن ــــــــــــــــــــــ

على مائدة في مطعم.

فوق قِمّة الشجرة.

في الزِّنزانة مع كريم.

٣ رحلات فوزي كلّها ــــــــــــــــــــــ

يوم الجمعة.

رحلات عمل.

حول الشجرة.

٤ كلّ أرباح شركة فوزي ــــــــــــــــــــــ

تعود إلى الشركة.

تذهب إلى المَأمور.

موجودة تحت الشجرة.

٥ ستجد فوزي على مَكتَبه ــــــــــــــــــــــ

يوم السبت فقط.

قبل السابِعة.

في زنزانة سمير.

٦ فوزي يأَخذ مُرَتَّبه فقط مثل ــــــــــــــــــــــ

حَمَلة الأسهُم.

كلّ الزملاء.

الغرفة التجاريّة.

Local flavors

orientalist	مُستَشرِق/مُستَشرِقون
Egyptologists	عُلَماء المِصريّات
sponsor	كَفيل/كُفَلاء
marriage official	مَأذون
imam	إمام/أَئِمّة
muezzin	مُؤَذِّن/مُؤَذِّنون
sheikh	شَيخ/شُيوخ
calligrapher	خَطّاط/خَطّاطون

Handy extras

And what does your son do now, Mrs. Anisa?	وماذا يفعل ابنك الآن يا مدام أنيسة؟
He cuts mens' hair in a famous barber shop.	إنّهُ يَقُصّ شَعر الرِّجال في مَحَلّ حَلاقة مَشهور.
He answers customers' questions in a call center.	إنّهُ يَرُدّ على أَسئِلة العُمَلاء في مَركَز اِتِّصال.
He prepares meat in a big butcher shop.	إنّهُ يُعِدّ اللَّحم في مَحَلّ جَزارة كَبير.
He sells plants in a garden centre.	إنّهُ يَبيع النَّباتات في مَشتَل زُهور.
He drives a school bus.	إنّهُ يَقود أوتوبيس مَدرَسة.
He has joined the navy.	إنّهُ اِنضَمَّ للأسطول.
And what about your daughter, Mrs. Anisa?	وماذا عن ابنتك يا مدام أنيسة؟
She's a nurse in the local hospital.	إنّها مُمَرِّضة في المُستَشفَى المَحَلّي.
She's the accountant and vet of a traveling circus.	إنّها مُحاسِبة وبَيطَريّة في سيرك مُتَجَوِّل.
She teaches mathematics to gifted children.	إنّها تُدَرِّس الرِّياضيّات للأطفال المَوهوبين.
She's in prison.	إنّها في السِّجن.
She runs a carpentry workshop.	إنّها تُدير وَرشة نِجارة.
She is the chef of a five-star restaurant.	إنّها شيف الطَّبّاخين في مَطعَم خمسة نُجوم.
And how was your day at the office, darling?	وكيف كان يومك في المَكتَب يا حبيبي؟
Wonderful! I got promoted today!	رائع! تَرَقَّيتُ اليوم! (تَرَقَّى/يتَرَقَّى)
Excellent! They gave me a pay rise.	مُمتاز! أعطوني زيادَة في المُرتَّب!
Amazing! I am now a partner!	مُدهِش! أَنا الآن شَريك!
Tar and asphalt! I lost my job.	زِفت وقطران! فَقَدْتُ وَظيفَتي.

Match the person to their logical place of work.

السجن/مشتل الزهور/الشارع/المطار/المستشفى/المدرسة/ورشة النجارة/السفارة

١ كلّ عملي بالخَشَب. ستجدني في _____

٢ أنا السفير وأعمل في _____

٣ أنا أعمل بالزَّفْت والقَطران. ستجدني في _____

٤ أنا المأمور وأعمل مع الضبّاط. ستجدني في _____

٥ أنا أعمل وسط النباتات الجميلة. ستجدني في _____

٦ أنا ممرّضة وأعمل في _____

٧ أنا أقود الأوتوبيس. أُحضِر الأولاد ثمّ أعود بهم. أعمل في _____

٨ كلّ عملي في الطائرة. ستجدني في _____

Now match these places of work to their logical person.

بيطريّ/قائِد سفينة/جزّار/مدير/عالم المِصريّات/طبّاخ شيف/حلّاق/مذيع

١ هنا أشهر مطعم في المدينة. هل أنت تبحث عن _____؟

٢ هنا قناة تليفزيون. هل أنتم تبحثون عن _____؟

٣ هنا الأسطول. هل جئتم لتبحثوا عن _____؟

٤ هنا أشهر محل حِلاقَة. هل تريد أن تعثر على _____؟

٥ أنت في وادي الملوك في الأقصر. هل تريدون أن تعثروا على _____؟

٦ هنا السيرك. هل أنت تبحث عن _____؟

٧ نحن نُعِدّ أحسن لحم في المدينة. هل أنتم تبحثون عن _____؟

٨ هذا مكتب مجلس الإدارة. هل أنت هنا لتبحث عن _____؟

I haven't got a desk! ‏ليس عندي مَكتَب!‏

unemployed	عاطِل/ عاطِلون
gardener	بُستانيّ/ بُستانيّون
fisherman	صَيّاد سَمَك/ صَيّادو سَمَك
painter	رَسّام/ رَسّامون
sculptor	نَحّات/ نَحّاتون
advertising representative	مَندوب إعلانات
salesman	بَيّاع/ بَيّاعون
broadcaster	مُذيع/ مُذيعون
translator	مُتَرجِم/ مُتَرجِمون
vet	بَيطَريّ/ بَيطَريّون
driver	سائِق/ سائِقون
policeman	شُرطيّ/ شُرطيّون
pilot	طَيّار/ طَيّارون
navigator	مَلّاح/ مَلّاحون
author	مُؤَلِّف/ مُؤَلِّفون
carpenter	نَجّار/ نَجّارون
iron smith	حَدّاد/ حَدّادون
hairdresser	حَلّاق/ حَلّاقون
traveling salesman	بَيّاع مُتَجَوِّل/ بَيّاعون مُتَجَوِّلون
journalist	صُحُفيّون/ صُحُفيّ
correspondent	مُراسِل/ مُراسِلون

EXERCISE 10·7

Circle the odd word out in this selection then write it down in the space provided.

١ شُرطيّ/مستشفى/ضابط _____

٢ حلّاق/طَيّار/مَلّاح _____

٣ بُستانيّ/مستشفى/شجرة _____

٤ زهرة/حَدّاد/نَجّار _____

٥ متجوِّل/يلفّ ويدور/نَحّات _____

٦ عاطِل/بَيطَريّ/لا يعمل _____

Other treasures كُنوز أُخرى

oilfield	حَقل نَفط/حُقول نَفط
barrel	بِرميل/بَراميل
drill	بَرّيمة/بَرّيمات
petroleum	بَترول
crude oil	زَيت خام
natural gas	غاز طَبيعيّ
refinery	مِصفاة/مَصافٍ
tank	صِهريج/صَهاريج
quarry	مَحجَر/مَحاجِر
mine	مَنجَم/مَناجِم
desalination plant	مَحَطّة تَحلية

It's action time

to drill (for oil)	نَقَّب/يُنَقِّب
to dig	حَفَر/يَحفُر
to refine	كَرَّر/يُكَرِّر
to export	صَدَّر/يُصَدِّر
to import	اِستَورَد/يَستَورِد
to invest	اِستَثمَر/يَستَثمِر
to supervise	أَشرَف/يُشرِف
to struggle	كافَح/يُكافِح
to supply	وَرَّد/يُوَرِّد
to vote	صَوَّت/يُصَوِّت
to elect	اِنتَخَب/يَنتَخِب
to select	اِختار/يَختار
to win	فاز/يَفوز
to postpone	أَجَّل/يُؤَجِّل
to delay	أَخَّر/يُؤَخِّر
to promise	وَعَد/يَعِد
to count	عَدّ/يَعُدّ
to support	أَيَّد/يُؤَيِّد
to oppose	عارَض/يُعارِض
to challenge	تَحَدَّى/يَتَحَدَّى
to protest	اِحتَجّ/يَحتَجّ
to influence	أَثَّر (في)/يُؤَثِّر (في)

Handy extras

The workers began their strike last Wednesday.	بدأ العُمّال إضرابَهُم يوم الأربعاء الماضي.
There is a conflict of interests between us.	هُناك تَعارُض في المَصالِح بَينَنا.
There is total equality between men and women in our company.	هناك مُساواة تامّة بين الرجال والنساء في شركتنا.
We will continue negotiating until we reach a final settlement.	سَنستَمِرّ في التَّفاوُض حتّى نَصِل إلى تَسوية نِهائية.
Our enemies are distorting the facts.	أعداؤُنا يُشَوِّهون الحَقائق.
They are spreading rumors and lies.	إنّهم يُرَوِّجون الإشاعات والأكاذيب.
I am being subjected to severe pressures.	أنا أتَعَرّض لضُغوط شَديدة جِدّاً.

Leap into politics القَفز إلى السِّياسة

party leader	زَعيمُ الحِزب
election campaign	حَملة انتِخابيّة/حَملات انتِخابيّة
publicity posters	مُلصَق دِعاية/مُلصَقات دِعاية
political party	حِزب سياسيّ/أحزاب سياسيّة
fortune	ثَروة/ثَروات
slogans	شِعار/شِعارات
tax	ضَريبة/ضَرائِب
personal life	حَياة شَخصيّة
mistress	عَشيقة/عَشيقات
scandal	فَضيحة/فَضائِح
greed	طَمَع
diplomatic answer	رَدّ دبلوماسيّ/رُدود دبلوماسيّة
eloquence	لَباقة
slip of the tongue	زَلّة لِسان
She cut the ribbon.	قَصّت الشَّريط.
He laid the corner stone.	وَضَعَ حَجر الأساس.
They gave the speeches.	ألقوا الخِطابات.
She planted this tree.	زَرَعَت هذه الشجرة.
He held the baby.	حَمَلَ الرَّضيع.
They unveiled the plaque.	أزاحوا السَّتار عن اللَّوْحة.
I object!	أنا أعتَرِض!
I deny everything.	أنا أُنكِر كُلّ شَيء.
We reject these methods.	نحن نَرفُض هذه الأساليب.

These allegations are baseless.

Disgraceful!

No comment.

هذه المَزاعِم لا أساس لها.

مُشين!

لا تَعليق.

EXERCISE
10·8

Now that Fawzi is rich and powerful, he prepares to go into politics. A team of political advisers teach him how to:

Cut the ribbon and plant a small tree. ١

تقصّ الشجرة وتأكل الحلوى الكبيرة.

تأكل الحلوى الصغيرة وتقص الشريط.

تقصّ الشريط وتزرع شجرة صغيرة.

Hold the baby and smile on television. ٢

تحمل التليفزيون وتصعد السلّم.

تحمل الرضيع وتبتسم في التليفزيون.

تحمل الرضيع والتليفزيون وتصعد السُّلَّم.

Say "These are baseless allegations!" when they are facts. ٣

تقول "هذه الأساسيات لا معنى لها!" وهي مزاعم.

تقول "هذه المَزاعِم لا أساس لها!" وهي حقائق.

تقول "هذه الحقائق لا معنى لها!" وهي تبتسم.

Deny everything. ٤

تقول كلّ شيء.

تنكر كلّ شيء.

لا تقول أيّ شيء.

Perfect the eloquent diplomatic answer that says nothing. ٥

تُتقِن الرَّدّ الدبلوماسيّ وتقول هذه الحقائق بلا معنى.

تقول كلّ شيء بالطريقة الدبلوماسيّة وهي حقائق.

تُتقِن الرَّدّ الدبلوماسيّ اللَّبِق الذي لا يقول أيّ شيء.

Avoid scandal and deny you have a mistress. ٦

تَتَجَنُّب الفضيحة وتُنكِر أن لك عشيقة.

تَتَجَنُّب العشيقة وتقول أَنك تَعشَق الفضيحة.

تَتَجَنُّب العشيقات وتجلس تحت الشجرة.

Fawzi's campaign manager is assigning duties to the staff. Select the logical ending.

١ أريد منكم بعض ملصقات الدعاية. اذهبوا إلى _____ (الخطّاط / الحلّاق / المستشفى)

٢ يجب أن يرى الناس صورة فوزي في كلّ مكان. ضَعوا صوره في كلّ _____ (المناجم / ورش النجارة / المجلات)

٣ أريد أن أرى إعلانات عن نشاط فوزي في كلّ _____ (الصهاريج / الشوارع / السجون)

٤ يجب أن يكون المصوِّر هنا حين يحمل فوزي _____ (الرضيع / مكتب المدير / الرجال والنساء)

٥ يجب أن يظهر فوزي في التليفزيون مساء اليوم وهو يقصّ _____ (الستار / الحساء / الشريط)

٦ تأكَّدوا أن المشتل سيُوَرِّد كميّات كبيرة من _____ (الفَضائح / المرّضات / الزهور)

Nadia Mansour is running against Fawzi in the next election. With her campaign manager, they prepare a press release. Read this extract.

إنّه زَمَن العَجائِب!

مَن بيّاع مجلات وجرائد إلى رئيس حِزب سِياسيّ كبير في عشر سنوات!

مجلات فوزي وقَنَواته تتحدّث عن نشاطه دون تَوَقُّف، ولكنّنا لا نعرف كيف، ولا من أين جاءَت ثَروته بهذه السرعة. أنا سَأَتَحَدّاه وسَأَقِف في طريقه. سَأَقول لكلّ الناس عن فَضائحه وأعماله المشينة. سَأَتَكلّم عن المُوَظَّفين في شَركاته الذين فَقَدوا وَظائِفهم وأصبَحوا عاطِلين بِسَبَب طَمعه وفَساده. سَأَتَحَدّث في خِطاباتي عن الصَفقات السوداء وراء السِّتار.

يَقول فوزي في حَملته أنه حَليف الرجل العادي في الشارع، ولكن هذا الرجل العادي لا يَعرف حَقيقة فوزي. يَجِب أن يعرف الرجل العادي لِمَن يُعطي صَوته. يَجِب أن يعرف الرجل العادي القِصّة الكامِلة.

اِنتَخَبوا نادية مَنصور، عُدوّ الفَساد رَقم واحد.

Select the Arabic that best represents the English.

The average man on the street. ١

الرجل العادي في الشارع.

الشارع الآخر بجوار البيت.

الرجل الأخير في وسط الشارع.

His magazines and his channels talk. ٢

قَنَواته تريد الحديث معكم.

مجلاته وقنواته تتحدّث.

حديثه وحياته هنا الآن.

Black deals behind the curtains. ٣

أبواب بيضاء وراء الصفقة.

صفقات سوداء وراء الستار.

ستار أسود وراء الباب الأبيض.

They talk non-stop. ٤

إنّهم يتحدّثون دون توقُّف.

لا تتحدّث ولا تتكلّم معهم.

إنّها تتوقّف ولكنّها لا تتحدّث.

They have become unemployed because of his greed. ٥

أصبحوا عاملين ولونهم أخضر.

الطمّاعين والعاملين يتحدّثون هنا.

أصبحوا عاطلين بسبب طمعه.

Where did it come from so fast? ٦

أين ذهبت ثروته في عشر سنوات؟

من أين جاءت بهذه السرعة؟

أين ذهبت السنوات بهذه السرعة؟

I will challenge you! ٧

أنا سأتحدّاه!

أنا سأتحدّاك!

هي ستتحدّاني!

She will stand in my way. ٨

سأقف في طريقه.

ستقف في طريقنا.

ستقف في طريقي.

Does not know the truth about Fawzi. ٩

لا يعرف حقيقة فوزي.

يعرف أن فوزي يقول الحقيقة.

لا يقول الحقيقة لفوزي دائماً.

EXERCISE 10·11

Answer these questions.

1. How long did it take Fawzi to go from newspaper boy to media tycoon?

2. Who is the number one enemy of corruption in this piece?

3. What do Fawzi's channels and magazines do non stop?

4. Who claims to be the ally of the average man on the street?

5. How does Nadia propose to expose Fawzi's black deals?

6. Where do Fawzi's black deals take place?

Select the English that best represents the Arabic.

١ رئيس حزب سياسي كبير.

His head is bigger than before.

Politics has gone to his head.

Head of a big political party.

٢ الحزب لا يعرف الحقيقة.

The truth is not an enemy.

The party does not know the truth.

This knowledge is not for parties.

٣ هل أنت عضو في هذا الحزب؟

Are you with this party of four?

Are you a member of this party?

Are you a member of this club?

٤ نصف المحاسبين فقدوا وظائفهم.

Half the jobs went to accountants.

Half the accountants lost their jobs.

Half the jobs were for accountants.

٥ صفقاتنا نظيفة وقانونيّة.

Our deals are clean and legal.

His curtains are clean and tidy.

It is legal to sign this deal now.

٦ لا تَعليق.

No comment.

Do comment.

I have nothing more to say.

Happy planet

الجُزء الحادي عَشَر: الكَوكَب السَّعيد

Looking up toward the sky at night, one of the most delightful features of the desert skies is how magnificent the stars look—except in a sandstorm.

Look above! اُنظُروا إلى أَعلى!

star	نَجم / نُجوم
moon	قَمَر / أَقمار
full moon	بَدر
crescent	هِلال
lunar	قَمَريّ
moonlight	ضَوء القَمَر
sun	شَمس
solar	شَمسيّ
sky	سَماء / سَماوات
planet	كَوكَب / كَواكِب
planet Earth	كَوكَب الأَرض
shooting star	شِهاب / شُهُب
space	الفَضاء
universe	الكَون
Milky Way	دَرب التَّبّانة
lunar eclipse	خُسوف
solar eclipse	كُسوف
north	شَمال
south	جَنوب
east	شَرق
west	غَرب

horizon	أُفُق/آفاق
horizontal	أُفُقيّ
vertical	رَأسيّ
gravity	الجاذِبيّة

Look around you! اُنظُروا حَولَكم!

environment	بيئة /بيئات
mountain	جَبَل/ جِبال
hill	تَلّ/ تِلال
rock	صَخرة/صُخور
valley	وادٍ/ وِديان
cave	كَهف/كُهوف
land	أَرض/ أَراضٍ
meadow	مَرج/مُروج
pastureland	مَرعَى/مَراعٍ
hole	حفرة /حفر
plateau	هَضَبة / هِضاب
mountain slopes	مُنحَدَرات الجبال
depression	مُنخَفَض/ مُنخَفَضات
desert	صَحراء / صَحارَى
river	نَهر/أَنهار
branch	فَرع / فُروع
current	تَيّار/ تَيّارات
flow	مَجرَى
lake	بُحَيرة /بُحَيرات
island	جَزيرة / جُزُر
coast	ساحِل/ سَواحِل
water spring	عَين ماء
swamp	مُستَنقَع/مُستَنقَعات
inlet	شَرم/شُروم
coral reefs	شُعاب مَرجانيّة

Local flavors

oasis	واحة/واحات
sand dunes	كُثبان رَمليّة
prayer for rain	صَلاة الاستِسقاء

Handy extras

The main road is to the east from here.	الطَّريق الرَّئيسيّ إلى الشَّرق مِن هُنا.
We will head north toward the capital.	سَنَتَّجِه إلى الشَّمال نَحوَ العاصِمة.
The southern coast is closer to us.	الساحِل الجَنوبيّ أَقرَب لَنا.
The river Nile flows from south to north.	يَجري نَهر النيل من الجَنوب إلى الشَّمال.

EXERCISE 11·1

You are a great explorer leading our party on a trip. Whenever we arrive at a particular natural feature you have to give us one of the following four instructions (in writing, in the space provided):

سَنَصعَد/سَنَنزِل/سَنَسبَح/سَنَمشي

١ وَصَلنا إلى بُحَيرة، _____ _____

٢ وَصَلنا إلى نَهر، _____ _____

٣ وَصَلنا إلى جَبَل، _____ _____

٤ وَصَلنا إلى حُفرة، _____ _____

٥ وَصَلنا إلى مُنحَدَرات، _____ _____

٦ وَصَلنا إلى تَلّ، _____ _____

٧ وَصَلنا إلى ساحِل، _____ _____

٨ وَصَلنا إلى وادٍ، _____ _____

٩ وَصَلنا إلى مَرج، _____ _____

١٠ وَصَلنا إلى هَضَبة، _____ _____

١١ وَصَلنا إلى مُنخَفَض، _____ _____

١٢ وَصَلنا إلى صَحراء، _____ _____

وَصَلنا إلى عَين ماء! سَنَشرَب! سَنَستَحِمّ!

Well done! At the spring we will drink and we will bathe!
Now it's time to plan the party's next move. Look at these notes:

الجَبَل والنَّهر إلى الغَرب من هُنا، والصَحراء والمُستَنقَعات إلى الشَّرق.

إلى الجَنوب من هنا هناك كَهف كبير يُمكِن أن نَنام فيه الليلة، و يُمكِن أن نَستَمِرّ في المَشي باتِّجاه الجَنوب على ضَوء القَمَر حتى نَصِل إلى ساحِل البَحر عندَ الفَجر ونَأخُذ السَّفينة من الميناء هناك.

ويُمكِن أن نَمشي نحو نَجم الشَّمال حتى نَصِل إلى الفَرع الشَّماليّ للنَهر.

هُناك سَنَطلُب من الصَّيادين أن يأخُذونا مَعهُم في مَراكِبهم.

اِتِّجاه مَراكِب الصَّيادين في الفَرع في الجَنوب الغَربيّ مع التَّيار حتّى يَصِلوا إلى مَجرَى النَّهر الرَّئيسيّ.

ومِن هناك يَستَمِرّون جَنوباً مع المَجرى الرَّئيسيّ حتى يَصِلوا إلى ساحِل البَحر.

EXERCISE
11·2

Now you've read the notes, and possibly drawn a rough sketch, decide what is true and what is false.

1. The swamps are to the west. (T/F)

2. Our destination is south. (T/F)

3. The river runs from east to west. (T/F)

4. We can spend the night in a hotel. (T/F)

5. The sea coast is to the south. (T/F)

6. We will try to be in the port by dawn. (T/F)

EXERCISE
11·3

Decide which English best represents the Arabic.

١ اِتِّجاهنا هو الجنوب الغربيّ

our direction is northwest

our direction is southeast

our direction is southwest

٢ سَنَستَمِرّ على ضوء القمر

we will continue by moonlight

they all need a two day break

we aim to be there before dawn

٣ فرع من فُروع النهر

two of the tree's branches

one of the river's branches

a tree branch by the river

٤ عند الفجر

by dawn

pray and go

before sunset

٥ الجبل والنهر والصحراء

the moon, the stars and a cave

the shooting star in the desert

the mountain, the river, and the desert

٦ نجم الشمال

the north pole

the northern star

keep going north

٧ مُمكن أن نستمرّ في المَشي

we can camp here tonight

we can continue walking

we can look for the cave

٨ سنطلُب من الصيّادين

we will ask the fishermen

they will catch some fish

we will continue fishing

٩ سنتّجه إلى الجنوب مع التيّار

we will head north through the desert

we will head east to avoid the swamps

we will head south with the current

١٠ سنَأخُذ السفينة من الميناء

they will camp outside the cave

we will take the ship in the port

we will reach the ship by dawn

EXERCISE
11·4

Now answer these questions about the exploration notes.

1. What two features are to the west of us?

2. Where is the cave from where we are?

3. What is the final destination of the fishermen's boats?

4. What directions do the fishermen's boats follow?

5. What two features are to the east of us?

6. Where might the party spend the night?

7. Why does our party want to go to the port?

It's action time حان وقت الأفعال

to shine	سَطَع / يَسطَع
to travel	سافَر / يُسافِر
to camp	خَيَّم / يُخَيِّم
to wander	تَـجَوَّل / يَتَجَوَّل
to fly	طار / يَطير
to take off	أَقلَع / يُقلِع
to land	هَبَط / يَهبِط
to sail	أَبحَر / يُبحِر
to row	جَدَّف / يُجَدِّف
to explore	إستكشَف / يَستَكشِف
to thaw	ذاب / يَذوب
to rust	صَدَأ / يَصدَأ

EXERCISE
11·5

Decide which Arabic best represents the English.

The sun is shining. ١

يَسطَع القمر هناك.

الشمس هي النجم.

تَسطَع الشمس.

The ship has sailed. ٢

سأَتَكَلَّم مع البَحّارة.

أَبحَرَت السفينة.

سنَبيع السفينة.

We will camp in the desert. ٣

أُحِبّ الصحراء والنُّجوم.

سنَمشي في الصحراء.

سنُخَيِّم في الصحراء.

They landed at the airport. ٤

هَبَطوا في المطار.

إشتَرَينا هذه الأرض.

الأرض هي المطار.

We wandered by the river. ٥

النهر هو نجم الشمال.

تَجَوَّلنا عند النهر.

سنُخَيِّم عند النهر.

We explored the desert. ٦

البُحَيرات في الصحراء.

إستَكشَفنا البُحَيرات.

إستَكشَفنا الصحراء.

Handy extras

weather	الطَّقس
climate	الجَوّ
moderate, sunny spring day	يوم رَبيعيّ مُعتَدِل ومُشمِس
summer is hot and dry in the daytime	الصَّيف حارّ وجافّ نَهاراً
cold and rainy in the fall	بارِد ومُمطِر في الخَريف
biting cold in winter	قارِس البُرودة في الشِّتاء

Sometimes, nature can be in a bad mood.

thunder	رَعد
lightning	بَرق
cloud	سَحابة/سُحُب
rain	مَطَر
wind	ريح/رِياح
fog	ضَباب
river overflowing	فَيضان النَّهر

Sometimes, nature can be in a very bad mood.

flood	سَيل/سُيول
storm	عاصِفة/عَواصِف
sandstorm	عاصِفة رَمليّة
earthquake	زِلزال/زَلازِل
drought	جَفاف
famine	مَجاعة/مَجاعات
epidemic	وَباء/أَوبِئة
hurricane	إعصار/أَعاصير
volcano	بُركان/بَراكين
volcanic eruption	ثَورة بُركان/ثَورات بَراكين
mud slide	اِنجِراف طينيّ/اِنجِرافات طينيّة
locusts	جَرادة/جَراد
natural disaster	كارِثة طَبيعيّة/كَوارِث طَبيعيّة

Local flavors

Khamaseen winds	خَماسين

Annual, hot, dusty, sandy and dry sandstorms that swoop across North Africa around Spring. They could last for a day or two each time. Not a fun feature.

The weather report brings either "Great news!" (خَبَر رائِع!) or "Bad news!" (خَبَر سّيِّء!)
Write down either one in the space provided, depending on what you think.

١ سَماء زَرقاء _____

٢ سُحُب رَماديّة _____

٣ إنجِراف طينيّ _____

٤ تَسطَع الشمس _____

٥ قارِس البُرودة _____

٦ ثورة البُركان _____

٧ إعصار _____

٨ يَسطَع البَدر _____

٩ عاصِفة رَمليّة _____

١٠ مُعتَدِل ومُشمِس _____

Waters المِياه

Pacific Ocean	المُحيط الهادِئ
Indian Ocean	المُحيط الهِنديّ
Atlantic Ocean	المُحيط الأطلَسيّ
Red Sea	البَحر الأحمَر
Dead Sea	البَحر المَيِّت
Mediterranean Sea	البَحر الأبيَض المُتَوسِّط
gulf	خَليج / خِلجان
ground water	مِياه جَوفيّة
mineral water	مِياه مَعدِنيّة
waterfall	شَلّال / شَلّالات
fresh water	مِياه عَذبة
source (river)	مَنبَع / مَنابِع
mouth (river)	مَصَبّ / مَصَبّات
stagnant water	مِياه راكِدة
polluted water	مِياه مُلَوَّثة
salt water	مِياه مالِحة
muddy water	مِياه عَكِرة

deep water	مِياه عَميقة
shallow water	مِياه ضَحلة
wave	مَوجة / أمواج
whirlpool	دَوّامة / دَوّامات

Local flavors

water wheel	ساقية / سَواقٍ
mirage	سَراب

EXERCISE
11·7

Select the appropriate word to complete the passage.

تَنحَدِر / المِياه / عُدنا / نُخَيِّم / سِتّة / اقتَرَبنا / يَومَين / حَمَلنا

قُمنا بِرحلة جميلة لِمُدّة _____ أيّام لِاستِكشاف مَنبَع النَّهر. _____ حَقائِبنا ومَشينا لِمُدّة يَومَين وكُنّا _____ في الصَّحراء. حين رَأينا المُستَنقَعات عَرَفنا أنّنا _____ مِن المَنبَع. وبعد قليل سَمِعنا صَوتاً غَريباً وكان هذا هو صوت _____ العَذبة وهي _____ مِن أعلى الجَبَل في مِنطَقة الشَّلّالات. خَيَّمنا هناك لِمُدّة _____ وكُنّا نَسبَح في المِياه العَميقة. وبعد ذلك _____ إلى العاصِمة. كانت رِحلة رائِعة!

EXERCISE
11·8

Decide which is the odd one out.

١ المِياه المالِحة / البحر / المِياه العذبة

٢ سَحابة / نَجم / الشمس

٣ كَوكَب / دَوّامة / الأرض

٤ بَدر / الصحراء / هِلال

٥ شلّالات / النهر / كُثبان رَمليّة

٦ سَمِعنا / اِشرَبوا / اُنظُروا

٧ إعصار / عاصِفة / يَصعَد

٨ سنَهبُط / سنَنزَل / سنَمشي

٩ أعلى الجَبَل / وراء الجبل / فوق الجبل

١٠ سنمشي نحو نجم الشمال / سنَتَّجِه إلى الشمال / سنُخَيِّم في الشمال

Join these two in logical units.

النهر	١ المُحيط
العَذبة	٢ مراكب
المَيِّت	٣ مَنبَع
كَوكَب الأرض	٤ البَحر
الهادِيء	٥ كُثبان
بُركان	٦ جاذِبِيَّة
رَملِيَّة	٧ المِياه
الصيادين	٨ ثورة

Animals الحَيَوانات

Lurking beneath the waves

It's nice to dip your toes into the water. But, mind that toe . . .

shark	سَمَكة القرش/أَسماك القرش
octopus(es)	أخطبوط
crab	سَرَطان البحر
crocodile	تِمساح/تَماسيح
eel	ثُعبان الماء/ثَعابين الماء
whale	حُوت/حِيتان
dolphin	دُلفين/دَلافين
sea turtle	سُلحُفاة بَحرِيّة/سَلاحِف بَحرِيّة
net	شَبَكة/شِباك

Animal tools

smell	الشَّمّ
hearing	السَّمَع
sight	البَصَر
feather	ريشة/ريش
wing	جَناح/أَجنِحة
beak	مِنقار/مَناقير
fin	زِعنِفة/زَعانِف

muscle	عَضَلة/عَضَلات
claw	مَخلَب/مَخالِب
horn	قَرن/قُرون
hoof	حافِر/حَوافِر
fang	ناب/أَنياب
jaw	فَكّ
tail	ذَيل/ذُيول

EXERCISE
11·10

Select the English that best represents the Arabic.

١ هذا التِّمساح يَنظُر إلينا!

Look at this crocodile!

This crocodile is looking at us!

I just saw a crocodile!

٢ أَنيابه تَشبَه المَوز.

His fangs look like bananas.

They don't like eating bananas.

I'd like to have a banana now.

٣ أَسماك القِرش تَلُفّ وتَدور.

He will turn into a shark.

I get dizzy when I eat fish.

Sharks spin and turn.

٤ هذه التَّماسيح لا تَتَحَرَّك.

The sight of crocodiles is very moving.

Crocodiles never look like they are moving.

These crocodiles are not moving.

٥ ثَعابين الماء كثيرة في هذا الخَليج.

I can see these eels are spinning.

There are a lot of eels in this gulf.

Eels can drink quite a lot of water.

٦ هل أَسماك القِرش تَشُمّ؟

Do I smell of shark?

Can sharks smell?

Does my shark smell?

٧ عَضَلات الفَكّ قَويّة جِدّاً.

Do not test their jaw strength.

I will muscle my way out of it.

Jaw muscles are very strong.

٨ السَّلاحِف البَحريّة لَيسَت سريعة.

Sea turtles are not fast.

Sea turtles eat quickly.

Sea turtles don't move.

٩ شِباك الصيّادين في المَركَب.

I can see the fishermen from my window.

The fishermen's nets are on the boat.

The fisherman is looking through his window.

١٠ المِياه هنا راكِدة ومُلَوَّثة.

Stagnant water is not always polluted.

The polluted water may be stagnant.

The water here is stagnant and polluted.

Animal health

the digestive system	الجِهاز الهَضميّ
the nervous system	الجِهاز العَصَبي
the reproductive system	الجِهاز التَّناسُليّ
the immune system	الجِهاز المَناعيّ
the respiratory system	الجِهاز التَّنَفُّسيّ
loss of appetite	فُقدان الشَّهيّة
skin rash	اِلتِهاب جلديّ / اِلتِهابات جلديّة

pregnancy	حَمل
birth	وِلادة
breast	ثَدي/أَثناء
breast-feeding	رِضاعة
bleeding	نَزيف
deteriorating	يَتَدَهوَر
extinct	مُنقَرِض

She is injured, and we can't save her.	إنّها مُصابة ولَن نَستَطيع أن نُنقِذها.
He is recovering quickly, and I'm optimistic.	إنّه يَتَعافى بِسُرعة وأنا مُتَفائِل.

EXERCISE

11·11

You are a biology teacher working with very young children on lesson one. Keep it simple! Select the appropriate Arabic word.

١ أين الأنياب؟ نعم! إنّها في ــــــــــــ (الفكّ/الجلد/الثدي)

٢ أين الريش؟ نعم! إنّه في ــــــــــــ (التِّمساح/الموز/الجناح)

٣ أين الحيتان؟ نعم! إنّها في ــــــــــــ (المُحيط/المياه مَعدِنيّة/الصُّخور)

٤ أين القرون؟ نعم! إنّها فوق ــــــــــــ (الجبل/الشمس/الرأس)

٥ أين يرضعون؟ نعم! هنا في ــــــــــــ (فكّ التمساح/ذيل السمكة/ثدي الأمّ)

٦ أين الديناصور؟ نعم! إنّه ــــــــــــ (مُنقَرِض/مُتَفائِل/تحت الجَناح)

EXERCISE

11·12

You did well in lesson one. Here's lesson two.

١ التَّماسيح الكبيرة تأتي لنا بالتماسيح الصغيرة. التماسيح الصغيرة تأتي من ــــــــــــ (السُّحُب/الأَجنِحة/الجِهاز التَّناسُليّ)

٢ الجهاز المَناعيّ لا يعمل. إنّها مُصابة ــــــــــــ (بثَورة بُركان/بِالتِهابات جلديّة/بالسمك)

٣ الحيتان الصغيرة تأتي بعد الحَمل والوِلادة لأن الحيتان لَيسَت ــــــــــــ (أسماكاً/صُخوراً/شبابيك)

٤ الجهاز العَصَبيّ سليم. عاد إليه ــــــــــــ (المياه العَذبة/السَّمع والبَصَر/الصيّادون)

٥ الأسماك الكبيرة تأكل الأسماك الصغيرة. الأسماك الصغيرة تذهب إلى ــــــــــــ (نَجم الشمال/الجهاز الهَضميّ/الشلّالات)

٦ أنا آسِف. النزيف قويّ ومُستَمِرّ. لن نستطيع أن _____ (نُخَيِّم/نُنقِذها/نُجَدِّف)

٧ أنا متفائِل الآن، ولكن قال البَيطريّ إنّه _____ (يَتَعافى/يَتَدَهوَر/يَنزِف)

٨ الأسماك لَيسَ لها مَخالِب ولا حَوافِر، ولكن لها _____ (أَجنِحة/زَعانِف/جاذِبيّة)

Tame أليف

dog	كَلب / كِلاب
muzzle	كِمامة / كَمائِم
cat	قِطَّة / قِطَط
horse	حِصان / أَحصِنة
parrot	بَبَغاء / بَبغاوات
tortoise	سُلحُفاة / سَلاحِف
rabbit	أَرنَب / أَرانِب
guinea pig	أَرنَب هِنديّ / أَرانِب هِنديّة
rare	نادِر
miniature	مُصَغَّر
rider	فارِس / فُرسان
horsemanship	فُروسيّة
saddle	سَرج / سُروج
horseshoe	جِدوة / جِدوات
riding boots	حِذاء رُكوب / أَحذِية رُكوب
helmet	خوذة / خوذات
stables	إسطَبل / إسطَبلات
nest	عُشّ / أعشاش

It's action time

to sting	لَدَغ / يَلدَغ
to pounce	انقَضّ / يَنقَضّ
to devour	الِتَهَم / يَلتَهِم
to dig	حَفَر / يحفُر
to gallop	بَرطَع / يُبَرطِع
to rein in	لَجَم / يَلجِم
to prepare (oneself)	استَعَدّ / يَستَعِدّ
to select	اختار / يَختار

to attack	هاجَم/يُهاجِم
to defend	دافَع/يُدافِع
to endure	تَحَمَّل/يَتَحَمَّل
to protect	حَمَى/يَحمي
to lay eggs	باضَت/تَبيض
to hatch	فَقَسَت/تَفقِس
to weigh	وَزَن/يَزِن
to train	دَرَّب/يُدَرِّب
to slow down	أَبطَأَ/يُبطِئ
to speed up	أَسرَع/يُسرِع
to race	سابَق/يُسابِق
to jump	قَفَز/يَقفِز
show jumping	قَفز السُّدود

Around the farm حَول المَزرَعة

cow	بَقَرة/بَقَر
bull	ثَور/ثيران
calf	عِجل/عُجول
sheep	خَروف/خِراف
ewe	نَعجة/نِعاج
lamb	حَمَل/حِملان
goat	ماعِز/مَواعِز
donkey	حِمار/حَمير
mule	بَغل/بِغال
fox	ثَعلَب/ثَعالِب
poultry	دَواجِن
worm	دودة/ديدان
flea	بُرغوث/بَراغيث
mosquito	بَعوضة/بَعوض
wasp	دَبّور/دَبابير
fly	ذُبابة/ذُباب
butterfly	فَراشَة/فَراشات
rat	جُرَذ/جِرذان

mouse	فَأر / فِئران
owl	بومة / أبوام
pigeon	حَمامة / حَمام
hawk	صَقر / صُقور
bat	وَطواط / وَطاويط
nightingale	بُلبُل / بَلابِل
kite	حَدَأة / حِدأ
straw	قَشّ

Local flavors

water buffalo	جاموسة / جَواميس
camel racing	سِباق الجِمال

Bingo is a working dog in a working farm. Here is a page from chapter one of his memoirs.

في الحَقيقة، أنا لا أَستَيقِظ لأنّني لا أَنام. عِندَنا هُنا في المَزرَعة قِطّة اسمها "لوسي" وهي تَستَطيع أن تَنام طَوال النَّهار. أنا لا أَعرِف كيف! ولَكِن أنا ... أنا مِثل العُضو المُنتَدَب في هذه المَزرَعة. لِماذا؟ لأن الحَيَوانات الأُخرى تَلُفّ وتَدور في كلّ مَكان وتَنسى نفسها. أنا أُعيدها إلى مَكانِها السَّليم وأُدافِع عَنها وأحميها طَوال النهار والليل. دَواجِن ... عُجول وأَبقار صَغيرة ... نِعاج وجِمالها التي تَرضَع ولا تَعرِف أي شيء عن الحياة الحَقيقيّة. أنا أَمشي وأَجري وأَسبَح وأَحفُر وأَشُمّ كلّ شيء، وهذا جُزء بَسيط من عَمَلي اليوميّ. أنا مَشغول جدّاً طوال الوقت، ولكنّني أُحب الحياة هنا جدّاً! إن حياتي هُنا هي أَجمَل حَياة في الكَون!

EXERCISE 11·13

Decide what is true and what is false.

1. Bingo believes lambs know nothing about real life. (T/F)

2. Bingo never wakes up because he loves sleeping. (T/F)

3. Lucy can sleep all day. (T/F)

4. The other animals go wandering. (T/F)

5. Bingo believes he is on duty 24/7. (T/F)

6. Lucy has to smell everything. (T/F)

Select the Arabic that best represents the English.

I don't know how! ١

أنا لا أعرف كيف!

هي لا تعرفني!

أنا أعرف من هنا!

I don't sleep. ٢

أنا لا أعرف.

أنا لا أستطيع.

أنا لا أنام.

She can sleep all day. ٣

هي تستطيع أن تنام طوال النهار.

هي لا تعرف أن هناك ليل ونهار.

كانت نائمة حين عُدنا في آخر النهار.

I am like the managing director. ٤

هذا هو المدير الذي أحبّه.

أنا مثل العُضو المُنتَدَب.

أنا لا أحبّ المدير الجديد.

These animals forget themselves. ٥

نسيتُ أربعة حيوانات مثلها.

هذه الحيوانات تَنسى نفسها.

هذا هو الحيوان الذي لا يَنسى.

I smell everything. ٦

أنا وأنت لا نشمّ.

أنا أشمّ كلّ شيء.

أنا لا أحبّ الكلاب.

my daily work ٧

عملي في جريدة

عملي اليوميّ

جريدتي لا تعمل

The best life in the universe! ٨

أجمل كلب في العالم!

أجمل حياة في الكون!

أكبر بنت في الجامعة!

EXERCISE 11·15

Select the English that best represents the Arabic.

عندنا جاموسة اسمها "جيجي". ١

We have a water buffalo named Lucy.

We have a water buffalo named Gigi.

Our water buffalo still loves the farm.

أمشي وأجري وأسبح وأحفر. ٢

I walk and run and swim and dig.

I bark and sleep like most dogs do.

I eat and drink but I don't sleep.

أنا أُعيدها إلي مكانها السليم. ٣

I return them to their owners.

I return them to the right place.

Their owners wanted them back.

أُدافع عنها وأحميها. ٤

I defend them and protect them.

A good lawyer will defend them.

We protect our patch with vigor.

٥ أنا أحبّ حياتي هنا جدًّا.

I too love Lucy a lot.

Gigi loves the farm very much.

I love my life here a lot.

٦ لماذا؟ لأنّه جزء من عملي اليوميّ.

When? Maybe today or tomorrow.

Who? The daily workers built it today.

Why? Because it is part of my daily work.

EXERCISE
11·16

Complete the Arabic.

١ وَضَعَ الفارس الجِدوة على باب _____ (المُحيط/الاسطبل/القطّة)

٢ عشّ البُلبُل فوق _____ (النهر/الشمس/الشجرة)

٣ إنقَضّ الثَّعلَب على _____ (الثور/الحمامة/التمساح)

٤ إلتَهمَت البومة _____ (المركب/الحوت/الفأر)

٥ هَبَطَ الصَّقر من السماء بِاتِّجاه _____ (الجُرَذ/القشّ/السرج)

٦ هذا الكهف فيه مليون _____ (مجلس إدارة/دلفين/وَطواط)

Handy extras

reptiles	زَواحِف
rodents	قَوارِض
crustaceans	قِشريّات
birds of prey	الطُّيور الجارِحة
prey	فَريسة/فَرائِس
predator(y)	مُفتَرِس

رِحلة السفاري Safari

giraffe	زَرافة/زَراف
rhino	خَرتيت
bear	دُبّ/دِبَبة
wolf	ذِئب/ذِئاب
lion	أَسَد/أُسود
lion cub	شِبل/أَشبال
hyena	ضَبع/ضِباع
gazelle	غَزال/غِزلان
elephant	فيل/أَفيال
hippopotamus	فَرَس النَّهر/أَفراس النَّهر
tiger	نَمِر/نُمور
leopard	فَهد/فُهود
flamingo	بَشَروشة/بَشَروش
pelican	بَجَعة/بَجَع
seagull	نَوْرَس
peacock	طاووس/طَواويس

EXERCISE 11·17

Arrange these animals by size, starting with the biggest.

١ برغوث/فيل/فهد

٢ دبّ/غزال/صقر

٣ بَعوضة/بَجَعة/فَرَس النهر

٤ جُرَذ/زرافة/ضَبع

٥ نَمِر/فأُر/شِبل

٦ وَطواط/خَرتيت/نَوْرَس

٧ ثوْر/حمامة/فراشة

٨ بُلبُل/حِمار/بومة

٩ أسد/ذِئب/دَبّور

١٠ طاووس/حصان/ذبابة

*Every environment or setting is followed by three groups of animals, one of which shouldn't
really be there. See if you can identify it.*

١ حديقة سفاري: أفيال/بِغال/أشبال

٢ مُستَنقَعات: بَشَروش/بعوض/دَواجِن

٣ المحيط الهادئ: خَرتيت/دلافين/حيتان

٤ البحر الأحمر: أسماك القرش/فئران/ثعابين الماء

٥ بيت الزُّواحِف: ثعابين/تماسيح/براغيث

٦ المزرعة: عُجول/أُسود/نعاج

٧ صحراء: غِزلان/سَلاحِف بَحريّة/جِمال

٨ كهف كبير: وَطاويط/ثعابين/زَراف

٩ اِسطَبل: بَبَغاء/أحصِنة/مُهر

١٠ حديقة بيتنا: قِطَط/ذِئاب/كلاب

Answer key

1 Home and town

1·1

1 Is Nadia on the balcony?

2 Is the apartment in this building?

3 All the windows are in one room.

4 The bedroom has a window and the sitting room has a balcony.

5 The elevator door is at the entrance of the building.

6 This external wall is between the entrance and the garden.

1·2

١ شَقّة.

٢ السَّلالِم.

٣ تُطِلّ.

٤ يُرَمِّمون.

٥ الحَديقة.

٦ السَّطح.

1·3

١ غَسّالة أطباق وفُرن وثَلّاجة: المطبخ

٢ بلّاعة ومِرآة وصُنبور: الحَمّام

٣ مِدفأة ومِروحة وأَريكة: غُرفة الجُلوس

٤ خَلّاط ومِقشّة ومائِدة: المطبخ

٥ سِتار وماسورة ومِحبَس: الحَمّام

٦ خِزانة وبَطّانيّة وسَرير: غُرفة النَّوم

1·4

١ غرفة النوم: بلّاعة

٢ غرفة الجلوس: جردل

٣ غرفة الطعام: صُنبور

٤ الصالة: مقشّة

٥ الحمّام: مكواة

٦ المطبخ: حمّام

٧ الشرفة: مرآة

٨ المدخل: غرفة طعام

٩ الحديقة: خلّاط

١٠ السطح: مدخل

١١ المصعد: غسّالة

١٢ حمّام السباحة: مصعد

1·5

He demolished the slums.

He restored the factories.

He modernized the playgrounds.

He repaired the dam.

He built the swimming pool.

He painted the bridges.

١ هَدَمَ العَشوائِيّات.

٢ رَمَّمَ المَصانِع.

٣ جَدَّدَ المَلاعِب.

٤ أَصلَح السَّدّ.

٥ بَنَى حمّام السباحة.

٦ دَهَنَ الجُسور.

1·6

١ سَتدهن التماثيل.
٢ سَتُجَدِّد مَركَز التَّسَوُّق.
٣ سَتُصلِح المَلاعِب.
٤ سَتُرَمِّم الفَنارة والطاحونة.
٥ سَتَبني المستشفى.
٦ سَتَشتَري التليسكوب الجديد للمِرصَد.

1·7

١ هُناك سيّارات وشاحنات كثيرة في الطريق في ساعة الذُروة
٢ قِسم الحَوادِث والطَّوارِئْ في المستشفى
٣ السيّارات في الطريق ولكن المُشاه على الرصيف
٤ تَستَخدِم سوزان القطار لأن بيتها في أطراف المدينة
٥ أنا في قاعة المَزادات لأنّني أُريد تَماثيل قديمة
٦ الأولاد في المَلجأ يُحِبّون الحديقة والمَلاعِب

1·8

١ الشبّاك والشرفة
٢ السلّم والجرس
٣ الفنارة والميناء
٤ المُشاه والإشارات
٥ المرآة والكرسيّ
٦ الجسر والسدّ

1·9

١ الكبابجيّ
٢ الحَلّاق
٣ بيت أمّي
٤ محلّ السيّارات
٥ المَصرِف
٦ المطار

1·10

١ بيتي جديد/بيتي قديم
٢ على يمين بيتي/على يسار بيتي
٣ خارج بيتي/داخل بيتي
٤ يبني بيتي/يهدم بيتي
٥ بيتي صغير/بيتي كبير
٦ قبل بيتي/بعد بيتي

2 Family and friends

2·1

٧ عيد الأمّ
٥ عمّي   ٣ خالتي   ١ زوج
٦ حفيد   ٤ حماتي   ٢ أمّ

2·2

١ I go to my grandfather's house by public transport.
٢ My husband is in the bank and my daughter is in the cinema.
٣ My grandmother went to the casino on her birthday.
٤ Our maternal aunt's apartment is above ours.
٥ My father, mother, brother, and sister are on the balcony.
٦ His mother-in-law will build this new fence for them.

2·3

١١ حاجِب (اثنان)   ٦ لِحية (واحدة)   ١ أَنف (واحد)
١٢ نَقن (واحدة)   ٧ وَجه (واحد)   ٢ جَبين (واحد)
١٣ رمش (عَدَد كبير)   ٨ جَفن (اثنان)   ٣ أُذُن (اثنان)
١٤ شارِب (واحد)   ٩ رَأس (واحدة)   ٤ عَين (اثنان)
١٥ فَكّ (اثنان)   ١٠ سِنّة (عَدَد كبير)   ٥ رَقَبة (واحدة)

2·4

١ I am searching for a tall young man.
٢ This young man is muscular with a dark complexion.
٣ This young man has broad shoulders and Eastern features.
٤ Do you have a big house in an upscale neighborhood?

2·5

1. Gigi thinks Ali is just what she's looking for. (F)

2. Ali works in a small law firm. (T)

3. Gigi doesn't care too much about material things. (F)

4. Ali drives to work every morning. (F)

5. Gigi appears to like men with beards. (T)

6. Ali's apartment is in the city center. (F)

2·6

٤ أنفهُ كبير.	١ هو رجل طويل.
٥ كان يَعرق كثيراً.	٢ له شارب كثيف.
٦ له وَجه أمين وابتسامة جذّابة.	٣ له شعر قصير مُجَعَّد ولحية طويلة.

2·7

٥ رجل بَخيل	٣ رجل جَشِع	١ رجل ثريّ
٦ فتاة أمينة	٤ فتاة قصيرة	٢ إمرأة فُضوليّة

2·8

٤ وافَقَت داليا لأنّها تُريد أَن تَتَزوَّج أحمد.	١ لا تُثَرثِر عَمّتي مع أبي.
٥ رَفَضَت عَمّتي وقالَت: لا تُناقِشني!	٢ وافَقَت خالتي.
٦ تُحِبّ سميرة شارِب زَوجها.	٣ كلّ عائلتي فُقَراء ويُخَلاء.

2·9

The words and their opposite:

٥ يَكرَه/يحب	٣ كَريم/بخيل	١ يَرفُض/يوافق
٦ زَواج/طلاق	٤ قصير/طويل	٢ نَحيف/بدين

2·10

٤ أُحِبّ في أبي... أنّه كريم وخفيف الدم.	١ أحمد رجل جَذّاب لأنه... طويل وخفيف الدم وكريم.
٥ تَكرَه حماتي... تَجاعيد الوَجه.	٢ تعيش داليا في نعيم لأن... خطيبها ثريّ وكريم ويُحِبّها.
٦ كلّ أصدقائي يُحِبّون أمّي لأنّها... كريمة وتُحِبّ الابتسام.	٣ كلّ الجيران يُحِبّون أنور لأنّه... كريم ويُحِبّ الجيران والمُناسَبات الاجتماعيّة.

2·11

١ على رصيف محطّة القطار. رجل طويل. شارب كثيف.

٢ مَدخَل المَلجَأ. إمرأة نحيفة. شعر قصير. أنف كبير.

٣ سَلالِم المُستَشفى. إمرأة قصيرة. وَشم كبير على رَقَبَتها.

٤ الثلاثة الآن مَعاً على رصيف الشارع. يُثَرثِرون خارج محلّ الجَوهرجي.

٥ يَدخُلون محلّ الجَوهرجي. في الداخل ثلاث دَقائِق.

٦ يخرجون من محلّ الجَوهرجي. يُسرِعون باتِّجاه سيّارة. تُسرِع السيّارة باتِّجاه النَّفَق.

٧ في النَّفَق. يَحجِب النفق كلّ شيء. سَأتناوَل الغداء الآن.

3   Describing this and that

١ لا توجَد شاحنات كبيرة على الجسر لأنّه ضَعيف وقَديم

٢ الأولاد يحبّون هذا المَلعَب لأنّه فَسيح وفارِغ

٣ سَألَ المُدَرّس الأولاد عن قُطر الدائرة

٤ يحبّ المُشاة هذا الرَّصيف لأنّه عَريض

٥ تُريد زَوجتي هذه الأريكة لأنّها مَتينة

٦ نُريد أثاثنا الآن لأن شقّتنا فارغة

3.2

١ عاموديّ/أُفُقي

٢ متين/ضعيف

٣ مُعَقَّد/بسيط

٤ على اليسار/على اليمين

٥ قصير/طويل

٦ مُلَوَّث/نَقيّ

٧ أماميّ/خَلفيّ

٨ مُنخَفِض/مُرتَفِع

٩ غامِض/واضِح

١٠ مَكشوف/مُغَطّى

3.3

١ مُغطّى

٢ الضَّحل

٣ مُستَديرة

٤ شائك

٥ المَسحوق

٦ عميق

3.4

١ محلّ الزهور

٢ أبيض وأسود

٣ خضراء وفسيحة

٤ شعرها أسود وعُيونها بنيّة

٥ سوداء

٦ الأسود والأخضر

3.5

soft apricot paste ١

waxy orange powder ٢

greasy fish tongue ٣

concentrated lemon juice ٤

pure green olives ٥

red, sticky flower sherbet ٦

This is a relative issue! ٧

3.6

I discovered it in my kitchen. ١

any car and any truck ٢

It suits all engines. ٣

I put all of this in the mixer (blender). ٤

This empty bucket is sturdy and transparent. ٥

liquid toothpaste ٦

3.7

١ مُحَرّك بسيط

٢ محرّك أماميّ

٣ محرّك خَفيّ

٤ محرّك متين

٥ محرّك مُغطّى

٦ محرّك بالحدّ الأقصى

٧ محرّك عريض

٨ محرّك بصَوت عالٍ

٩ محرّك مُعاصِر

١٠ محرّك بحَرَكة ناعمة

محرّك مُعَقَّد

محرّك خلفيّ

محرّك ظاهر

محرّك ضعيف

محرّك مكشوف

محرّك بالحدّ الأدنى

محرّك ضَيِّق

محرّك بصَوت مُنخَفِض

محرّك قديم

محرّك بحَرَكة خَشِنة

3·8

١ ضاحية مرغوبة ومَطلوبة. شارع عريض. الجدران الخارجيّة بيضاء.

٢ الحديقة لها شَخصيّة ظاهرة. الكثير من الزهور.

٣ مَدخَل خاف لحمّام السباحة، و ملعب الأطفال والتنس.

٤ سَلالِم من الرخام. الأبواب والشبابيك خضراء. تَماثيل في الشُرفات الواسعة.

٥ سقف مرتفع. الخشب مكشوف. مدفأة.

٦ حجرة الجلوس شاسعة. تُقَسَّم؟ تُفْصَل؟

٧ مطبخ بيضاوي. حمّامات مستديرة.

٨ نادرة. مبلغ معقول. أنا أُوافِق.

3·9

١ المَدخَل.
٢ المطعم.
٣ المطبخ.
٤ حمّام السباحة.
٥ المخزن.
٦ الثَلّاجة.

3·10

1. I am a rare and desirable woman. We were living in paradise.

2. My husband demolished everything. A big love and a sturdy marriage.

3. Her head is flat. The mirror, the television, and the telephone are her ceiling.

4. His mother told me he was generous and wealthy.

5. She was graceful, attractive, and full of femininity.

6. These are all simple matters.

3·11

1. Hoda thinks Majid has destroyed their marriage. (T)

2. Majid thinks Hoda has a towering intellect. (F)

3. Hoda believes their marriage is solid. (F)

4. All of Majid's family were keen on Hoda. (F)

5. Majid used to ask Hoda to marry him about seven times a day. (T)

6. Majid's mother told Hoda that he was rich and generous. (T)

7. Hoda and Majid will live happily ever after. (F)

3·12

١ شخصيّتي عميقة، ولكنها ناعمة وطريّة.

٢ أنا إمرأة نادرة، رشيقة وجذّابة.

٣ ستجدها هناك، تثرثر في التليفون.

٤ الآن، تَكَشَّفَت الأمور.

٥ هل هو ثريّ وكريم أم فقير وبخيل؟

٦ أنا سأهدم هذا البيت المتين!

4 Time

4·1

١ السَّمّاك مُغلَق يوم الأَحَد، وهو مُغلَق اليوم. غداً هو يوم الاثنين.

٢ أنا أزور أمّي كل يوم جُمعة لـمُدّة ساعتَين. أنا زرتُ أمّي أمس. اليوم هو يوم السبت.

٣ اليوم هو الأربعاء، ونحن في المساء. غداً هو يوم الخميس.

٤ أنا أَستَخدِم السيّارة يوم السبت. سَأَستَخدِمها غداً. اليوم هو يوم الجمعة.

٥ كُلّ أُسبوع أَذهب إلى سوق الخُضار يَوم الاِثنين. أنا كنت هناك اليوم. أمس كان يوم الأحد.

٦ يَبدَأ شَهر رَمَضان غداً. أوّل يوم هو الخميس. اليوم هو يوم الأربعاء.

4·2

١ أَذهَب إلى النادي مرّة في الأسبوع...

٢ ولكنّي لا أَذهب أبداً يوم الأحد.

٣ أين المُدير؟ خَرَجَ مُنذ خمس دقائق.

٤ ولكنّه سيَرجِع خلال ساعة.

٥ يُؤَدّي أَغلَب المُسلمين فَريضة الحَجّ مرّة في العمر.

٦ يبدو أن الرّحلة ستَستَمِرّ إلى الأبد.

٧ لَمْ أرَ مَحَطّة بَنزين منذ ساعتين.

٨ لَنْ نَصِل أبداً!

00:00	مُنتَصَف اللَّيل
05:30	الفَجر
10:30	الصَّباح
12:00	الظُّهر
14:30	بعد الظُّهر
19:00	الغُروب
19:30	الشَّفَق
21:30	المَساء

4·4

أبدَأ يومي في الصباح الباكِر. بعد صَلاة الفَجر مُباشرة، أَذهَب إلى المَطبَخ وأَتَناوَل الإفطار. أنطَلِق في سيّارتي إلى المَطار في أَطراف المدينة وأَعمَل هُناك حَتّى المَساء. ثم أَتَّجِه إلى بيتي. يوم الجُمعة أُحِبّ أن ألعَب التنس الساعة الثالثة بعد الظُّهر مع أُختي سميرة.

4·5

أخيرا	١ أوَّلاً
الغروب	٢ الشروق
في الظلام	٣ في وضح النهار
في دفعة واحدة	٤ بالتدريج
وقت غير مناسب	٥ وقت مناسب
على المدى الطويل	٦ حالا
أوّل النهار	٧ آخِر النهار
من وقت إلى آخَر	٨ باستمرار

4·6

1. Anwar saw Nadia on a Friday around three o'clock in the afternoon about four or five months ago.

2. He was by the window when he first saw her.

3. He said it was long, soft, and black.

4. She was playing tennis with another girl.

5. In his living room.

6. The first step is to buy her some flowers.

7. The second step is to ask her out to lunch.

8. On Sunday.

4·7

Yesterday, he was at the barber to cut his hair and beard. ١

Today, he went to the flower shop early in the morning, before breakfast. ٢

He bought lots of red, yellow, and blue flowers. ٣

Anwar is now sitting on the sofa in front of the wall clock. ٤

Anwar is about to go out at any moment. He's going toward the door! ٥

Anwar has returned to the sofa. He postponed everything to next Friday. ٦

٤ لا نُريد الضُّيوف في بيتنا،
ولكنّنا سنُعطي لكلّ ضَيف زَيتونة.

٥ تحبّ جيهان الجُلوس في غرفتها،
ولكنّها تذهب إلى المطبخ أو الحمّام من وقت إلى آخر.

٦ إسماعيل عنده بيت كبير في الضَّواحي،
سَتَجِده هناك عند حمّام السِّباحة.

١ سيَتَناوَل حَسَن الغَداء في الشُّرفة،
ثمّ يَجلِس على الأريكة لمُدّة ساعتَين.

٢ أرجوكُم! لا تُضَيِّعوا وَقتي.
أنا لا أُحِبّ الجيران والأُسرة والأصدِقاء.

٣ يذهب إبراهيم إلى الخَبّاز في الظلام،
بعد غُروب الشمس.

٤ النَّفَق مُغلَق يوم الجمعة حاوِل يوم السبت.

٥ المَرحَلة الأُولى كانت أمس، ولكن المَرحَلة الإضافيّة غداً.

٦ تَأَخَّرتُ قليلاً. عاد إلى بيته منذ خمس دقائِق فقط.

١ هذه مناسبة نادرة جدّاً. إنّها مَرّة في العُمر.

٢ أَسرَعَ في سيّارته الجديدة في اتِّجاه الجسر.

٣ أرجوكم! لا تُضَيِّعوا وَقتكم أنا لا أُحِبّ الحفلات.

Completed English

We will wait here until sunset. ١

I've wanted to become an engineer all my life. ٢

I'll tell you everything at a suitable time. ٣

The stage of adolescence is a difficult stage in the life of a person. ٤

I'll come back tomorrow with my birthday certificate. ٥

Were you just about to go out immediately? ٦

٤ أنور، هذه مناسبة نادرة، مرّة في العمر.

٥ عَلِّق كلّ شيء وإذهَب إلى المدخل في الثالثة.

٦ لا تجلس على الأريكة وحاوِل أن تأتي في الموعِد!

١ أنور، الأسبوع القادم هو أسبوع خاصّ جدّاً.

٢ اِذهَب إلى المَشتَل يوم الجمعة في الصباح الباكر.

٣ اِشتَرِ الكثير من الزهور. حمراء وصفراء وزرقاء.

5 Eating and drinking

٥ دَجاج وبَطاطِس مُحَمَّرة

٦ لَحم

٧ بيتزا

١ سَمَك

٢ زُبد

٣ خُبز

٤ طَماطِم

macaroni with minced meat

white cheese with black olives

chicken grilled over charcoal

fresh vegetables from the market

raw fish with Japanese rice

omelet with fresh parsley

١ مكرونة مع اللحم المفروم

٢ جُبن أبيض مع الزيتون الأسود

٣ الدجاج المشوي على الفحم

٤ الخضروات الطازجة من السوق

٥ سمك نيّء مع الأرزّ اليابانيّ

٦ أومليت مع البقدونس الأخضر

marinated chicken stuffed with carrot and parsley ٤

minced meat with cheese and dried parsley ٥

home made falafel with smoked onion omelette ٦

macaroni with minced meat and tomato sauce ١

organic eggs with garlic and thyme ٢

slices of grilled fish with celery and fresh coriander ٣

5.4

١ بيضة	٣ سمك	٥ ملح
٢ بقدونس	٤ مكعّبات	٦ جزر

5.5

١ قَطِّع الجزر ثمّ قَشِّر البطاطس!

٢ قَلّب المرق وأنت تُكَثِّف صلصة الطماطم!

٣ ٤ لا تُضيف الثوم قبل أن تُخفِّف الطماطم أوّلاً!

٤ أُبشُر الجبن قبل أن تَحشو الدجاج!

٥ أعطني شرائح الدجاج وأفرُم هذا اللحم بسرعة!

٦ اِغسَل ثمّ حَمِّص هذه الخضروات وأنت تَشوي هذه السمكة!

5.6

1. In the oven.
2. No, the carrots are boiled and the potatoes are fried.
3. Parsley, minced meat, and fried onions.
4. Spaghetti with tomato sauce with cheese and fresh coriander.
5. The meat is flavored with garlic, thyme and olive oil.
6. Oil, lemon, and fresh orange slices.
7. The kitchen is closed, but the restaurant serves only pizza.

5.7

١ أنا أحبّ السمك المشوي. سأذهب يوم السبت

٢ أنا أحبّ الاسباجيتي. سأذهب يوم الخميس

٣ أنا أحبّ البورجر. سأذهب يوم الثلاثاء

٤ أنا لا أحبّ البيض. لن أذهب يوم الأربعاء

٥ أنا أحبّ الأرزّ. سأذهب يوم الجمعة

٦ أنا أحبّ البيتزا. سأذهب يوم الأحد

٧ أنا أحبّ الدجاج. سأذهب يوم الأثنين

5.8

١ ذَهَبتُ إلى السوق في الصباح الباكر.

٢ اِشتَرَيتُ خضروات المَوسِم ودجاجة كبيرة.

٣ عُدتُ إلى البيت وذَهَبتُ إلى المطبخ.

٤ غَلَيتُ بعض الماء والملح وبصلة في حَلّة كبيرة.

٥ قطّعتُ الدجاجة ووَضَعتُها في الماء المَغلي.

٦ غَسَلتُ وقطّعتُ الخضروات ثمّ أضَفتُها للدجاجة.

٧ تَرَكتُ الحلّة على نار هادِئة لمدّة ساعة ونصف.

٨ بعد ذلك، كان الحَساء جاهِزاً للأكل.

5.9

١ طازَج، مُجَمَّد، مُدَخَّن أو مُجَفَّف

٢ جاهِز للأكل فَوراً

٣ اُترُكوه ليغلي لمدّة خمس دقائق

٤ قَدِّموه مع الأرزّ أو المكرونة

٥ أضيفوا البصل المحمّر، والثوم ومَرَق الدجاج

٦ قَطّعوا البقدونس الأخضر والكرفس والكزيرة

٧ اِنقَعوا اللوز مع البندق في وِعاء كبير

5.10

قهوة بالحليب	قهوة بدون حليب
كوب ماء بارد	كوب ماء ساخن
شاي خفيف	شاي ثقيل
زجاجة بيرة صغيرة	زجاجة بيرة كبيرة
كولا بالثلج	كولا بدون ثلج
قهوة سادة	قهوة سكّر زيادة
كوب نبيذ أحمر	كوب نبيذ أبيض

5·11

Table one: ١
3 x bottles of cola
1 x fresh orange juice
1 x bottle of water

Table two: ٢
6 x bottles of lemonade
1 x sugarcane juice
1 x cup of iced tea

Table three: ٣
1 x bottle of beer
3 x plates of french fried potatoes
1 x hot chocolate
4 x glasses of lemon juice with lemon slices

Table four: ٤
1 x cup of tea with milk
1 x cup of Turkish coffee with extra sugar
1 x mint tea
1 x glass of white wine

Table five: ٥
1 x glass of water with an orange slice
1 x an empty glass
1 x a cup of green tea with no sugar

Table six: ٦
3 x the weekly special for three
1 x a glass of tomato juice with salt and pepper

5·12

١ تَسَوَّقتُ صباح اليوم واشتريتُ ستّ دجاجات من السوق.

٢ سأَشوي ثلاث دجاجات على الفحم، وسأَطبخ ثلاث دجاجات في الفرن.

٣ سأُقدِّم الدجاج مع بعض المكرونة بصلصة الطماطم والجبن المبشور.

٤ سأُقدِّم لضيوف جيهان الكولا بالثلج و عصير البرتقال والآيس كريم.

5·13

1. The greedy customer had a long neck. (F)
2. He sat at table number seven by the door. (F)
3. He ordered a lot of dishes, including fried fish. (T)
4. He ordered two different plates of macaroni. (T)
5. The greedy customer appears to like potatoes a lot. (T)
6. There were bits of basil stuck to his beard. (F)
7. Mimi is planning to have chicken for lunch today. (T)

6 Education

6·1

١ أنا اِسمي نادر وعُمري الآن واحد وعشرون سَنة

٢ في البداية، ذَهَبتُ إلى رَوضة أطفال قريبة جدّاً من البيت

٣ ولأنّها قريبة، كُنتُ أمشي إلى هُناك مع أُمّي في الصباح

٤ وبعد ذلك ذَهَبتُ إلى مدرسة اِبتدائيّة في حَيّ أَبعَد قَليلاً

٥ ولأنّها أبعَد، كُنتُ أذهَب مع أبي في الصباح بالسيّارة

٦ ولكن حين ذَهَبتُ إلى مدرسة ثانويّة في حَيّ بعيد جدّاً عن بيتنا

٧ تَعَلَّمتُ كيف آخُذ المُواصَلات العامّة إلى مدرستي يوميّاً

٨ وبعد المَدارس دَخَلتُ الجامعة وأَخَذتُ شهادة في الكومبيوتر

٩ أُريد أن أَستَمِرّ في دراسة الكومبيوتر وآخُذ الدكتوراة

١٠ وبعد ذلك سَيكون اِسمي دُكتور نادر. إنّه زَمَن العَجائب!

6·2

١ يَجمَع المُمَرِّض التَبَرُّعات للمُستَشفى الجديد

٢ سَتَكون دار الحضانة الجديدة مُفيدة جدّاً للمُجتَمَع

٣ المُفَتِّشون يُريدون الاِجتِماع مع كلّ المُدَرِّسين والمُدَرِّسات

٤ أنا أَخَذتُ شهادة الدكتوراة والآن مُحاضِر في الجامعة

٥ يا نادية! هذا وقت المُذاكَرة والمُراجَعة، اُترُكي الجيتار جانباً

٦ هناك إجماع بين كلّ المُدَرِّسين أنَّني سَأخُذ الدَّرَجات النِّهائيّة

6.3

1. This nurse combines kindness with speed.
2. This group came from one school and one class.
3. Their town has one small institute for teaching Sociology.
4. Mounir collects old cars and has a large collection of them.
5. This director studied cinema with us at Berlin University.
6. I want to study the sciences that benefit society.

6.4

١ تُدَرِّس الدكتورة جيهان لنا علم الاجتِماع يوم الثلاثاء.

٢ في الفصل، يُفَكِّر نادر دائماً في نادية.

٣ يُذاكِر أولاد عَمَّتي بعد الإفطار.

٤ الرياضيّات يا إسماعيل من أَهَمِّ الموادّ الإجباريّة.

٥ منير لا يَسأَل ولا يُناقِش ولا يُفَكِّر.

٦ الإجماع هو أن بشير سَيأخُذ الدَّرَجات النِّهائيّة.

6.5

١ شهادة الدكتوراة في عُلوم الكمبيوتر

٢ يدرُس اللغة العربيّة في مَعهَد بعيد عن بيته

٣ الامتحانات سَتَبدَأ في الأسبوع القادم

٤ العُمّال هناك كلّهم مُتَطَوِّعون

٥ لم أَدرُس اللّغة الفَرَنسيّة في المدرسة

٦ رَسَبَت في خمسة موادّ من ستّة

6.6

1. Mario has a shiny new Italian sports car. (F)
2. The institute where he studies Arabic is near the port. (T)
3. The dean is called Dr. Zeinab. (F)
4. Mario revises the plurals before lunch. (F)
5. Dr. Moussa teaches Italian to Chinese students. (F)
6. At night, Mario raids the fridge for something simple to eat. (T)

6.7

١ يبدأ نَهاري في السابعة

٢ تُحِبّ المُدَرِّسة أُسلوبي في الكتابة

٣ أنا طالب في معهد دراسات اللغة الفرنسيّة

٤ أنا أُراجِع الجمع بعد الظُهر

٥ القاموس دائماً في سيّارتي

٦ أحياناً أَسأَل العميد

٧ تَشرَح مُدَرِّستي كلّ شيء في الفصل

6.8

1. Mario starts his day at six thirty.
2. Mario always has the dictionary and reference books by his side.
3. Dr. Zeinab likes to smile as she explains things in class.
4. The big lighthouse and the port are the two landmarks near the institute.
5. Mario eats lunch in an Italian restaurant.
6. He usually orders macaroni (pasta) with tomato sauce.
7. Mario spends his evenings on the sofa, watching old Egyptian black and white movies, and eating spaghetti or any other simple food from the fridge.

6.9

عزيزي السيّد أبو النور،

تحية طيّبة،

إنجازات ابنكُم مُذهلة يا سيّد أبو النور. (منير)

يا سيّد أبو النور، إنّنا نَبحَث عن حل لبعض مُشكِلات ابنكُم. (حسين)

إن رأسه ليس هنا، ولكن في مكان آخر بعيد. (حسين)

إنّه طَموح، ويحبّ المدرسة ويريد أن ينجَح. (منير)

إنّه يرفُض المشاركة، ولا يريد أن يَتَعَلَّم كيف يُغَيِّر أسلوبه السلبيّ. (حسين)

إنّه يُناقِش ويسأل وله عَقل فُضوليّ. أسئلَته عميقة وأسلوبه جذّاب وناعم. (منير)

إنّه يكرَه الفصل، ويريد أن يكون في الشُرفة أو الشارع أو على السُّلَّم أو بجوار المدخل. (حسين)

إنه يُثَرْثِر باستمرار، ولِسانه طويل ولا يُرَكِّز في الحِصَص. (حسين)

إنه يسير في طريق له اتِّجاه واحد: النجاح والجامعات الكبيرة. (منير)

إنه يَتَّجِه نحو الرُسوب.لا يمكن أن يَستَمِرّ معنا لأنَّه يُضَيِّع وقته ووقتنا. (حسين)

مع تَحيات إدارة المدرسة،

سكرتير عامّ المدرسة

6.10	٦ اِستَمَرَّ أربع ساعات	٤ تُراجعون في البيت	١ لَم تُذاكِر
	٧ لالغَدّ.	٥ النِّهائيّة	٢ عَلامة بعد السُّؤال
			٣ مُشكِلة في الفصل

6.11

١ يَدرُس فصل مسز مايفلاور شكسبير وديكنز هذه السنة.

٢ أسلوب زكريا في الكتابة بالانجليزيّة ممتاز لأنه واضح وسَلِس.

٣ لا تُريد مسز مايفلاور أن يَكتُب منير في الهامِش.

٤ مسز مايفلاور ترى أن سليم يَحتاج إلى دُروس إضافيّة.

٥ يدرس فصل مسز مايفلاور "يوليوس قيصر" يوم الثلاثاء.

٦ نادية رمزي تَشطُب كلمات كثيرة على الصفحة.

٧ تريد مسز مايفلاور من الفصل أن يُلَخِّص ديكنز يوم الإثنين.

٨ تَرى مسز مايفلاور أن رشيد عنده بعض المشاكل في البيت.

٩ يَدرُس فصل مسز مايفلاور المُرادِفات يوم الأربعاء.

١٠ يوم الخميس هو يوم المُراجَعة لأن الامتِحان في الأسبوع القادم.

7 Traveling and exploring

7.1	٨ السويد	٥ تونس	١ سويسرا
	٩ المغرب	٦ مصر	٢ فنزويلا
	١٠ اليونان	٧ السعوديّة	٣ فرنسا
			٤ تايلاند

7.2	٦ أثينا	٤ الرياض	١ باريس
	٧ لندن	٥ القاهرة	٢ بغداد
			٣ الدوحة

7.3

١ أنا اسمي أحمد. أنا عِراقيّ وأُقيم في مدينة بغداد وهي عاصِمتنا.

٢ جَواز سفري عراقيّ، وأنا سأُسافِر إلى الولايات المتحدة لزيارة عَمَّتي في ولاية فلوريدا.

٣ مَلَأتُ الاستمارة وأَرسَلتُها إلى السفارة.

٤ تأشيرَتي صالِحة لزيارة واحدة فقط.

٥ سَتَتَوَقَّف طائرَتي في باريس عاصمة فرنسا لمُدّة ثلاث ساعات.

٦ بعد ذلك سَنَطير مُباشَرةً إلى واشنطن عاصمة الولايات المتّحدة.

٧ ومِن هناك سأخُذ طائرة أصغر إلى ميامي لأن عَمَّتي تعيش فيها.

٨ تُريد عَمَّتي أن تأخُذني إلى أكابولكو في المكسيك ولكن هذا مَعناه أنَّني سأحتاج إلى تأشيرة أُخرى!

7.4	٥ في ميناء مَرسيليا	٣ صالِحة لمُدّة ستّة شهور	١ بجوار الشِبّاك
	٦ في وسط العاصمة	٤ لِتَزوروا ولاية كاليفورنيا	٢ خمس محطّات

7·5	٥ القُنصُليّة	٣ الميناء	١ عريضة
	٦ حقائبهم	٤ سنُقلِع	٢ المطار

7·6
٥ أخذنا حقائبنا إلى الغُرَف.
٦ ذهبنا إلى المطعم لتَناوُل العشاء.
٧ مشينا في حدائق المُنتَجَع بعد الأكل.
٨ رجعنا إلى الغرف لننام.

١ ربطنا أحزِمة الأمان اِستِعداداً للهُبوط.
٢ هبطَت بنا الطائرة في المطار.
٣ أخذنا باصا سياحيّا من المطار إلى الفندق.
٤ ملأنا الاِستِمارات في قِسم الاِستِقبال.

7·7
أخذنا الطائرة لنطير إلى مصر لنَقضي إجازَتنا في الصَّحراء. أخذنا مَعنا الخِيام لنَنام فيها. رَكِبنا سيّارة خاصّة واتَّجَهنا إلى أعماق الصحراء. قُدنا سيّارَتنا فوق التِلال وبين كُثبان الرِّمال لمُدّة تسع ساعات إلى أن وَصَلنا إلى الواحة، هناك نَصَبنا الخِيام ونِمنا حتّى الصباح. قَضَينا خمسة أيّام رائعة، رَكِبنا الجِمال بالنَّهار، وفي الليل جَلَسنا حول النار نُغَنّي ونَتَكَلَّم ونَضحَك ونَنظُر إلى النُّجوم اللامِعة في السماء. كانَت رحلة رائعة!

7·8
خَبَر رائِع! خَبَر سَيِّء!

٥ خَبَر سَيِّء!	٣ خَبَر رائِع!	١ خَبَر رائِع!
٦ خَبَر رائِع!	٤ خَبَر سَيِّء!	٢ خَبَر سَيِّء!

7·9

4 She took my passport, phone, and some dollars.

5 I am now sitting on the sidewalk of a big street.

6 I haven't eaten anything except half a celery stick.

1 I went on a tour to visit the sites.

2 Our ship has disappeared with our suitcases.

3 An attractive girl approached me.

7·10

4 I'm on the sidewalk and my fingers are frozen.

5 I asked for help from the consulate.

6 The procedures will take four working days.

1 The captain of the ship has sailed.

2 Her features are attractive and she's funny.

3 She was funny, but 'light of hand' too.

7·11

1. Khalil left the cruise ship to go on a tour and visit the sites.

2. He returned to the city center to look for a hotel.

3. The person who offered to help him was a tall, funny girl who seemed rich and had attractive features. She was also light of hand!

4. Khalil kept his passport, his phone, and some dollars in his little bag.

5. Khalil was sitting on the sidewalk to write this postcard.

6. The last thing he's eaten was half a celery stick which he found in a glass on a sidewalk restaurant table.

7. He expects to fly home in about four days time.

7·12

1 The attractive star smiled at me and said, "You're funny!"

2 The whole group are from the same generation.

3 All tourist class seats were reserved so I sat in first class.

4 She asked to come with me on my trip to the oasis.

5 Between you and me, I agreed in less than an instant!

6 Fifi takes two hours a day to prepare for her movie.

7 We sit around the fire to eat a grilled meal.

7·13

1. Samir used all his savings to buy a first class ticket for this flight. (F)

2. On the plane, Samir sat next to a beautiful movie star. (T)

3. The beautiful movie star thought Samir had no sense of humor whatsoever. (F)

4. Samir asked Fifi Abuyousif if she would like to join him on his desert safari. (F)

5. Most of the guests at the desert resort were of similar age. (T)

6. Fifi Abuyousif spent two hours every day preparing for her new film role. (T)

7. Fifi and Samir had separate tents, and enjoyed the resort's daytime activities together. (T)

8. Fifi and Samir ate their evening meals that were grilled on either charcoal or wood. (T)

9. Samir can't wait to get back home. (F)

10. In a broad sense, Samir has been quite lucky on this trip. (T)

7·14

١ فنجان شاي. ٤ خفيف الظلّ! ٦ بيتي

٢ السفينة اختفت. ٥ النجوم في السماء ٧ سبع فَوائِد.

٣ فرق شاسِع جدًّا!

8 Shopping and selecting

8·1

١ هل هذا هو المَقاس المُناسِب لي؟ ٤ هل هذا جِلد مَحَلّيّ؟

٢ هل هذا صوف أم قُطن؟ ٥ هل عندك اقتِراحات؟

٣ أين القِسم الرجاليّ؟ ٦ هل هذا الحِجاب من الحَرير والقُطن؟

8·2

١ أحمد في القسم الرجاليّ لأنّه يَحتاج إلى بعض الملابس الجديدة

٤ هذه البَضائِع أَغلى كثيراً لأنّها شُغل يَدويّ

٢ هذه البَضائِع من الصوف لأن مَوسِم الشِّتاء اقتَرَبَ

٥ ليس هذا الحِزام مَقاسي لأنّه كبير الحَجم

٣ هذه البَضائِع أرخَص كثيراً لأنّها مُستعمَلة

٦ إنّها في واجِهة المَحَلّ لأنّها بضائِع جديدة وجميلة وجذّابة

8·3

١ عَرض أزياء ٣ قَرارات ٥ عندي سيارة

٢ واجِهة المَحَلّ ٤ دجاج مشوي ٦ قَهوتي

8·4

١ على الأقَلّ/على الأكثَر ٤ محلّيّ/مُستورَد ٦ جاهز/تفصيل

٢ رَخيص/غالٍ ٥ حريميّ/رجاليّ ٧ جديد/مُستعمَل

٣ تُجّار التَجزِئة/تُجّار الجُملة

8·5

١ نعم، السعر مَعقول، ولكن أنا لا أحتاج إلى قميص جديد.

٢ في نهاية المَوسِم لن تَجِدوا كلّ المقاسات.

٣ يريد الوكيل دُفعة مُقَدَّمة قبل الشَّحن.

٤ أُنظُروا إلى التَلَف! أنا اشتَرَيتُها هنا يوم الخميس الماضي!

٥ ما هي تَكاليف التَّغليف والتَّوصيل؟

٦ إن كانَت عَيّنة مَجّانيّة، سآخُذ عشرة.

8·6

1. The reduced price on suitcases is available for one week only. (F)

2. Mansour appears to be a compulsive buyer. (T)

3. The man by the door bought the last Igloo Park refrigerator. (T)

4. Mansour desperately needs a new television set today. (F)

5. The sales girl nearly always smiles. (T)

6. Delivery of a new Igloo Park refrigerator will cost extra. (F)

8·7
1. Mansour visited the department store to buy a television set.
2. The black suitcases were priced at their wholesale price.
3. The blue fans are economic, sturdy, and reasonably priced.
4. Thirteen television sets. Nine in his apartment, and four in a warehouse on the roof.
5. He has an Igloo Park refrigerator in every room
6. The last television set was sold five minutes ago.

8·8

٦ عندي واحدة في كلّ غرفة.

٧ اِشتَرى آخر جهاز.

٨ خدمات مجانيّة.

٩ إنّها اِقتِصاديّة ومشهورة.

١٠ لماذا لا تريدين أَن تُعطيني حقيبة؟

١ إنّه عرض مغرٍ!

٢ نبيع هذه الحقائب السوداء.

٣ سعر الجملة

٤ يجب أَن تُسرِعِ!

٥ هناك فرصة نادرة.

8·9

This man is the agent and distributer. ٥

I have nine in the warehouse on the roof. ٦

What did you say about these blue suitcases? ٧

We have a tempting offer on television sets today. ١

It's a rare opportunity to buy a washing machine. ٢

The white suitcases are at the wholesale price. ٣

Maybe eight fans or nine. ٤

8·10

Don't forget these bottles. ٦

The cost of the raw material is high. ٧

You are welcome any time. ٨

We don't haggle. ٩

They adorn and embellish. ١٠

We know how to distill. ١

The most famous perfumer in the city. ٢

My whole family works with me. ٣

These are the trade secrets. ٤

The prices don't suit everyone. ٥

8·11

٦ ولكن، في النِّهاية

٧ مرحباً في أَيِّ وَقتٍ

٨ يُحاولون أَن يُقَلِّدونا

٩ العُطور المُقَلَّدة

١٠ لا تُقارَن

١ المرحوم جَدّي

٢ أَشهَر عَطّار

٣ حَوالي خمس وسبعين

٣ في الحقيقة، أُسرتي كلّها

٥ غالية قليلاً

8·12
1. Nearly all Ahmed's family work in the perfume business. (T)
2. Brenda has had a look around the store to check out some prices. (T)
3. Ahmed lives with his grandfather above the store. (F)
4. The perfume business appears to have well guarded trade secrets. (T)
5. Ahmed does not admit that his products are a little expensive. (F)
6. Ahmed believes his original perfumes are beyond comparison. (T)

8·13

١ ساعة ذهب /كيلو موز /زِرّ قميص رجاليّ

٢ زُمُرُّدة /قَفَص مانجو /بصلة

٣ سجادة صوف شغل يدويّ /دجاجة مشويّة /جُوال قديم مُستَعمَل وفارغ

٤ قميص رجاليّ مُفَصّل من الحرير الطبيعيّ /فنجان قهوة بالحليب والسكّر /كوب ماء بدون ثلج

٥ تذكرة طائرة في الدرجة الأولى حول العالم /بدلة رقص شرقيّ /نصف عود كَرَفس

٦ بعض الأحجار الكريمة /بعض الزّيتون /بعض الحَطَب

The small camels are made of leather. ٦

luxury, natural silk ٧

adding some details ٨

He paid the entire amount in cash. ٩

He smiled and didn't haggle. ١٠

I used to be a sailor. ١

One day, a beautiful girl from Russia came to me. ٢

I bought this shop from my late father-in-law. ٣

instead of the regular spangles ٤

Egyptian cotton is always in demand. ٥

8·15

1. Farouk's wife is called Nadia.

2. Farouk was a sailor before he bought the store.

3. The little souvenir camels are made of leather stuffed with sponge.

4. The tailors work six days a week.

5. The most popular item in the store is Egyptian cotton.

6. The girl asked for luxury, natural silk.

8·16

٥ جَهَّزْتُ مَبلَغا كبيرا

٦ فتاة جميلة من روسيا

٣ نَشكُر اللَّه

٤ أصداف نادِرة مُستَورَدة

١ بَدَلًا من التِرتِر العادِيّ

٢ دَفَعَ المَبلَغ كلَّه

9 Law, crime, and justice

9·1

٥ الخُروج من السِجن

٦ مَجهول

٣ لا يوجد دَليل

٤ بَصماتك على السِّلاح

١ بَريء

٢ حادِث مُرور بسيط

9·2

After I killed her her they arrested me in an ambush. Injustice! ١

I strangled him first, and then I kidnapped him. ٢

He provoked me so I stabbed him. ٣

She is not a real embezzler. She was going to give everything back. ٤

Now I have a weapon and a license, so I'll kill him on Tuesday. ٥

Is there any clemency for three crimes of murder and one crime of rape? ٦

9·3

new tires for my car ٦

I strangled him then I stabbed her. ٧

the exit gate ٨

I couldn't go through ٩

He was standing in my way ١٠

if you are innocent ١

I am a victim ٢

my neighbor is a rich lady ٣

if there were justice ٤

you'll be out of jail today or tomorrow ٥

9·4

٥ طَعَنَني بِخَنجَره المسموم.

٦ أخَذتُ المبلغ الذي أحتاجه.

٧ أين العَدالة يا ناس؟!

١ ماذا تفعل هنا؟

٢ كانت سيِّدة غنيّة جدّاً.

٣ عندنا ستائر قديمة في حجرة الجلوس.

٤ هي تريد إطارات جديدة لسيّارتها.

9·5

1. They met in a prison cell.

2. Samir needed to buy new curtains for the living room.

3. Samir asked his rich neighbor for money.

4. Karim works in a bank.

5. The bank manager stood in front of Karim's car.

6. Poison was the extra ingredient added to their daggers.

9.6
1. Karim and Samir are innocent victims. (F)

2. Samir and Karim are partners in a law firm. (F)

3. Karim helped himself to sack-loads of cash and gold. (T)

4. Samir strangled his neighbor. (T)

5. Karim and Samir will probably pay small fines. (F)

6. Karim was driving toward the exit when he saw the manager. (T)

7. Karim and Samir use a similar technique in dealing with rejection. (T)

9.7

١ مُكافأة للجريمة المُنَظَّمة!

مدينَتنا الآن عاصِمة غَسيل الأموال في العالَم.

٢ هل العَدالة مُغلَقة يوم الجمعة

سَطو مُسَلَّح في مطعم صباح يوم الجمعة.

٣ اِغتِصاب مدينتنا يَستَمِرّ

العِصابات المُسَلَّحة اِشتَرَت شَوارِعنا الآن.

٤ مَحكَمة أم سيرك؟

رجل مُلَثَّم يَعتَدي على الشُّهود.

٥ القَبض على ضَحيّة الجريمة!

غَرامة لِصاحِب سيّارة بثلاثة إطارات

٦ المُختَلِس سيَخرُج!

رجل البيتزا بريء من سَرِقة العَجين

9.8

٥ إنّهم يَسرَقون حقائب السُّوّاح

٦ البُيوت التي كانت مَرغوبة

٧ لا نَخرُج بعد غُروب الشمس

٨ هذه الجَريدة هي صَوت الحَقيقة.

١ نحن نَعيش في دائِرة من الخَوف

٢ هل العَدالة في إجازة؟

٣ أين ضُبّاط الأمن؟

٤ الضَّواحي التي كانت مَطلوبة

9.9
1. Cars disappear from in-demand neighborhoods.

2. Armed gangs roam the streets all night and all day.

3. Furniture disappears from desirable homes.

4. Tourists' bags go missing from the port quay.

5. The editor's family stops going out at sunset.

6. Passenger seats get stolen from the train station.

9.10

٥ الخِنجَر

٦ يُعامِلك بالرَّأفة

٣ مُلَفَّقة

٤ في الشَّوارِع

١ بِلا رُخصة

٢ القاضي

9.11

٥ الشَّمس

٦ الإرهاب والتَّطَرُّف

٣ وَقَفَ ضِدّ الفَساد

٤ مَلَكيّ

١ مُشاغِب

٢ وَلي العَهد

9.12
1. Mohsin is a republican and a troublemaker. (T)

2. Karim tried to blow up the atomic energy building. (F)

3. The guy they call "the doctor" is also a barber. (F)

4. Karim knows the difference between nuclear and solar energy. (F)

5. Anwar talks a lot. (T)

6. Karim enjoys chatting with the foreign sabotage specialist. (F)

9.13
1. Shawky hates the authorities.

2. Ibrahim wants solar energy only because it is clean.

3. Shawky is the number one enemy of the state security officers.

4. Mohsin wants a republican regime because he doesn't like the king.

5. Karim thought "analyst and commentator" meant "barber."

6. Karim approves of the king because he is amusing and has colorful clothes.

1. In truth, I don't know the difference.
2. He says he is a political activist.
3. You are the enemy of state security officers.
4. My troublemaker friends don't like the king.
5. He tried to sabotage something.
6. She is a specialist in espionage, terrorism, and sabotage.

١ العَنبَر الغَربيّ	العَنبَر الشَّرقيّ
٢ بعد الصَّلاة	قبل الصَّلاة
٣ اتِّفاق شَفويّ	اتِّفاق مَكتوب
٤ مُتَشَدِّد	مُتَساهِل
٥ يخرُج من الزِّنزانة	يعود إلى الزِّنزانة
٦ ظُروف عَاديّة	ظُروف استِثنائيّة

1. Demonstrations and mutiny inside the prison are exceptional circumstances.
2. We have written this official report and will present it to the warden.
3. The security officers condemn any corruption or bribery within the prison walls.
4. You will find the political prisoners in the Eastern wing.
5. In the end, we reached a verbal agreement.
6. It seems to me that the rebels have specific demands.

٥ المَأمور؟	٣ صَلاة الفَجر	١ حُقوقنا
٦ اتِّفاق	٤ الزِّنزانات	٢ نُفوذ

10 Business and politics

٧ رَئيس	٥ وَسيط	٣ مُحاسِب	١ مَجلِس
	٦ تَسويق	٤ بَاحثون	٢ مؤسِّس

٥ المحاسب يعرف الأرقام لأنّها مهمّة.
٦ نشاطنا قانونيّ وسليم.
٧ الشركة تدفع المرتَّبات والمزايا.
٨ هذا المبلغ ليس كبيراً جدّاً.

١ بيان الرئيس قصير.
٢ الإنتاج يَجِب أن يَزيد.
٣ المذكِّرة مكتوبة للرئيس.
٤ أعضاء المجلس أعدائي ما عدا محمّد رَمزيّ.

٥ احتكار	٣ الأرباح أعلى	١ نفقاتي كثيرة
٦ صفقة العام	٤ مُوجَز مُختَصَر	٢ يرتّبون الميزانية

٥ قبل السابعة.	٣ رحلات عمل.	١ يبيع المجلات.
٦ كلّ الزملاء.	٤ إلى الشركة.	٢ قِمّة الشجرة.

10·5	٧ المدرسة. ٨ المطار.	٥ مشتل الزهور ٦ المستشفى	٣ ستجدني الشارع ٤ السجن	١ ورشة النجارة ٢ السفارة
10·6	٧ جزّار ٨ مدير	٥ عالم المِصرِّيات ٦ بيطريّ	٣ قائِد سفينة ٤ حلّاق	١ طبّاخ شيف ٢ مذيع
10·7		٥ نَحَّات ٦ بَيطَريّ	٣ مستشفى ٤ زهرة	١ مستشفى ٢ حلاق

10·8

١ تقصّ الشريط وتزرع شجرة صغيرة.
٢ تحمل الرضيع وتبتسم في التليفزيون.
٣ تقول "هذه المَزاعِم لا أساس لها!" وهي حقائق.
٤ تنكر كلّ شيء.
٥ تُتقِن الرَّد الدبلوماسيّ اللَبِق الذي لا يقول أيّ شيء.
٦ تَتَجَنَّب الفضيحة وتُنكِر أن لك عشيقة.

10·9		٥ الشريط ٦ الزهور	٣ الشوارع ٤ الرضيع	١ الخطّاط ٢ المجلات

10·10

١ الرجل العادي في الشارع.
٢ مجلاته وقنواته تتحدّث.
٣ صفقات سوداء وراء الستار.
٤ إنّهم يتَحَدّثون دون توقُّف.
٥ أصبحوا عاطلين بسبب طمعه.
٦ من أين جاءت بهذه السرعة؟
٧ أنا سأتحدّاك!
٨ ستقف في طريقي.
٩ لا يعرف حقيقة فوزي.

10·11

1. It took Fawzi ten years to go from newspaper boy to media tycoon.
2. Nadia Mansour is the number one enemy of corruption in this piece.
3. Fawzi's channels and magazines talk about his activities nonstop.
4. Fawzi says he is the ally of the average man on the street.
5. She will make speeches to expose Fawzi's black deals.
6. Fawzi's black deals take place behind the curtain.

10·12

Half the accountants lost their jobs. ٤	Head of a big political party. ١
Our deals are clean and legal. ٥	The party does not know the truth. ٢
No comment. ٦	Are you a member of this party? ٣

11 Happy planet

11·1

٧ وَصَلنا إلى ساحِل، سَنَسبَح	١ وَصَلنا إلى بُحَيرة، سَنَسبَح
٨ وَصَلنا إلى وادٍ، سَنَنزِل	٢ وَصَلنا إلى نَهر، سَنَسبَح
٩ وَصَلنا إلى مَرج، سَنَمشي	٣ وَصَلنا إلى جَبَل، سَنَصعَد
٠١ وَصَلنا إلى هَضَبة، سَنَصعَد	٤ وَصَلنا إلى حُفرة، سَنَنزِل
١١ وَصَلنا إلى مُنخَفِض، سَنَنزِل	٥ وَصَلنا إلى مُنحَدَرات، سَنَنزِل
٢١ وَصَلنا إلى صَحراء، سَنَمشي	٦ وَصَلنا إلى تَلّ، سَنَصعَد

11·2

1. The swamps are to the west. (F)
2. Our destination is south. (T)
3. The river runs from east to west. (F)
4. We can spend the night in a hotel. (F)
5. The sea coast is to the south. (T)
6. We will try to be in the port by dawn. (T)

11·3

the Northern star ٦
we can continue walking ٧
we will ask the fishermen ٨
we will head South with the current ٩
we will take the ship in the port ١٠

our direction is south-west ١
we will continue by moonlight ٢
one of the river's branches ٣
by dawn ٤
the mountain, the river, and the desert ٥

11·4

1. The mountain and the river are to the west of us.
2. The cave is to the south from where we are.
3. The sea coast is the final destination of the fishermen's boats.
4. The fishermen's boats go south west then south.
5. The desert and the swamps are to the east of us.
6. The party might spend the night in a cave or walking in the desert.
7. Our party wants to go to the port to take the ship.

11·5

٥ تَجَوَّلْنا عند النهر. 　　٣ سنُخَيِّم في الصحراء. 　　١ تَسطَع الشمس.

٦ اِستَكشَفنا الصحراء. 　　٤ هَبَطوا في المطار. 　　٢ أَبحَرَت السفينة.

11·6

خَبَر رائِع / خَبَر سيّء

٦ ثورة البُركان　　خَبَر سيّء 　　١ سَماء زَرقاء　　خَبَر رائِع

٧ إعصار　　خَبَر سيّء 　　٢ سُحُب رَماديّة　　خَبَر سيّء

٨ يَسطَع البَدر　　خَبَر رائِع 　　٣ اِنجِراف طينيّ　　خَبَر سيّء

٩ عاصِفة رَمليّة　　خَبَر سيّء 　　٤ تَسطَع الشمس　　خَبَر رائِع

١٠ مُعتَدِل ومُشمِس　　خَبَر رائِع 　　٥ قارِس البُرودة　　خَبَر سيّء

11·7

قُمنا برحلة جميلة لِمُدّة سِتّة أَيّام لاستِكشاف مَنبع النَّهر. حَمَلنا حقائِبنا ومَشَينا لِمُدّة يَومَين وكُنّا نُخَيِّم في الصَّحراء. حين رأَينا المُستَنقَعات عَرَفنا أَنّنا اِقتَرَبنا من المَنبَع. وبعد قليل سَمِعنا صَوتاً غَريباً وكان هذا هو صوت المِياه العَذبة وهي تَنحَدِر من أَعلى الجَبَل في مِنطَقة الشَّلّالات. خَيَّمنا هناك لِمُدّة يومَين وكُنّا نَسبَح في المِياه العَميقة. وبعد ذلك عُدنا إلى العاصِمة. كانت رِحلة رائِعة!

11·8

٦ سَمِعنا
٧ يَصعَد
٨ سنَمشي
٩ وراء الجَبَل
١٠ سنُخَيِّم في الشمال

١ المِياه العذبة
٢ سَحابة
٣ دَوّامة
٤ الصحراء
٥ كُثبان رَمليّة

11·9

٥ كُثبان　　رَمليّة 　　١ المُحيط　　الهادِيء

٦ جاذِبيّة　　كَوكَب الأرض 　　٢ مراكب　　الصيادين

٧ المِياه　　العَذبة 　　٣ مَنبَع　　النهر

٨ ثورة　　بُركان 　　٤ البَحر　　المَيِّت

11·10

١ This crocodile is looking at us!
٢ His fangs look like bananas.
٣ Sharks spin and turn.
٤ These crocodiles are not moving.
٥ There are a lot of eels in this gulf.
٦ Can sharks smell?
٧ Jaw muscles are very strong.
٨ Sea turtles are not fast.
٩ The fishermen's nets are on the boat.
١٠ The water here is stagnant and polluted.

11·11

١ الفكّ
٢ الجناح
٣ المُحيط
٤ الرأس
٥ ثدي الأمّ
٦ مُنقَرِض

11·12

١ الجهاز التَناسُليّ
٢ بِالتهابات جلديّة
٣ أسماكاً
٤ السَّمع والبَصَر
٥ الجهاز الهَضميّ
٦ نُنقِذها
٧ يَتَعافى
٨ زَعانِف

11·13

1. Bingo believes lambs know nothing about real life. (T)
2. Bingo never wakes up because he loves sleeping. (F)
3. Lucy can sleep all day. (T)
4. The other animals go wandering. (T)
5. Bingo believes he is on duty 24/7. (T)
6. Lucy has to smell everything. (F)

11·14

١ أنا لا أعرف كيف!
٢ أنا لا أنام.
٣ هي تستطيع أن تنام طوال النهار.
٤ أنا مثل العُضو المُنتَدَب.
٥ هذه الحيوانات تَنسى نفسها.
٦ أنا أشمّ كلّ شيء.
٧ عملي اليوميّ
٨ أجمل حياة في الكون!

11·15

١ We have a water buffalo named Gigi.
٢ I walk and run and swim and dig.
٣ I return them to their right place.
٤ I defend them and protect them.
٥ I love my life here a lot.
٦ Why? Because it is part of my daily work.

11·16

١ وَضَعَ الفارس الجِدوة على باب الاسطبل
٢ عشّ البُلبُل فوق الشجرة
٣ انقَضّ الثّعلَب على الحمامة
٤ التَهمَت البومة الفأر
٥ هَبَطَ الصّقر من السماء باتِّجاه الجُرَذ
٦ هذا الكهف فيه مليون وَطواط

11·17

١ فيل/فهد/برغوث
٢ دبّ/غزال/صقر
٣ فَرَس النهر/بَجَعة/بَعوضة
٤ زرافة/ضَبع/جُرَذ
٥ نَمِر/شِبل/فأر
٦ خَرتيت/نَورَس/وَطواط
٧ ثَور/حمامة/فراشة
٨ جِمار/بومة/بُلبُل
٩ أسد/ذِئَب/دَبّور
١٠ حصان/طاووس/ذبابة

11·18

١ حديقة سفاري: بِغال
٢ مُستَنقَعات: دَواجِن
٣ المحيط الهادئ: خَرتيت
٤ البحر الأحمر: فئران
٥ بيت الزُّواحِف: براغيث
٦ المزرعة: أُسود
٧ صحراء: سَلاحِف بَحريّة
٨ كهف كبير: زَراف
٩ اسطَبل: بَبَغاء
١٠ حديقة بيتنا: ذِئاب